Embracing
ANXIETY

ALSO BY KARLA McLAREN

The Language of Emotions:
What Your Feelings are Trying to Tell You

The Art of Empathy:
A Complete Guide to Life's Most Essential Skill

The Dynamic Emotional Integration® Workbook

Escaping Utopia: Growing Up in a Cult, Getting
Out, and Starting Over (with Janja Lalich)

Embracing
ANXIETY

How to Access the Genius
of This Vital Emotion

KARLA McLAREN, M.ED.

sounds true
BOULDER, COLORADO

Sounds True
Boulder, CO 80306

This book is not intended as a substitute for the medical recommendations of physicians, mental health professionals, or other healthcare providers. Rather, it is intended to offer information to help the reader cooperate with physicians, mental health professionals, and health providers in a mutual quest for optimum well-being. We advise readers to carefully review and understand the ideas presented and to seek the advice of a qualified professional before attempting to use them.

Published 2020

Cover design by Lisa Kerans
Book design by Kate Kaminski, Happenstance Type-O-Rama

Printed in the United States

Library of Congress Cataloging-in-Publication Data

Names: McLaren, Karla, author.
Title: Embracing anxiety : how to access the genius of this vital
    emotion / Karla McLaren, M.Ed.
Description: Boulder, CO : Sounds True, 2020. | Includes bibliographical
    references and index.
Identifiers: LCCN 2019036844 (print) | LCCN 2019036845 (ebook) | ISBN
    9781683644415 (trade paperback) | ISBN 9781683644422 (ebook)
Subjects: LCSH: Anxiety. | Mental health. | Self-reliance.
Classification: LCC BF575.A6 M375 2020 (print) | LCC BF575.A6 (ebook) |
    DDC 152.4/6—dc23
LC record available at https://lccn.loc.gov/2019036844
LC ebook record available at https://lccn.loc.gov/2019036845

10 9 8 7 6 5 4 3 2 1

For my dear friend anxiety,
who has been misnamed, disrespected,
and pathologized — but who shows up
every day to help us, nonetheless.

And for you who long to live in ease
and harmony with your anxiety,
I welcome you.

Thank you for bringing your emotional
genius to your anxiety, and
to our waiting world.

Contents

PART III
Supporting Your Anxiety in the World

Exercises and Practices

Introducing
My Friend Anxiety

Emotions are at the center of everything you are: every relationship, every dream, every failure, every triumph, every act of violence, and every act of love. Your emotions are not just random sensations or meaningless moods — your emotions are vital to your intelligence, your social skills, and your ability to understand yourself and the world around you. Each of your emotions has a specific purpose, and each emotion brings you a unique set of gifts, skills, and genius. Your emotions are your guardians, your support system, and your friends, and you can learn how to work with all of them, brilliantly. Anxiety, the task-completion expert of your psyche, is no exception.

This book is a love letter to my friend anxiety. Anxiety does so much for us, but sadly, it's usually treated as a problem or a disease. There are many reasons for this. One is that we haven't been taught to treat our emotions as necessary parts of our intelligence. Another is that emotions tend to be looked down on as less valuable than our so-called rationality (or our spirituality). Yet another reason is that many people experience anxiety as a painful and overwhelming emotion that doesn't seem to have any value. Because of these and many other reasons, we're usually taught to overlook anxiety's gifts and focus only on its flaws, and it's hard to love something we see as a flaw. Therefore, the first thing we'll do in this book is embrace anxiety so that we can approach it in a new way and learn how to love it. *Really.*

Most of us have been taught to feel ashamed about or afraid of our anxiety, or to treat it as a sign of weakness or trouble. Some people even talk about anxiety as an epidemic, as if it's a serious disease that's also contagious. This is a shame because anxiety is an essential emotion with an important job to do: it helps us look ahead, organize ourselves, and gather the energy we need to get things done. As with any other emotion, however, anxiety can become unbalanced, uncomfortable, and even overwhelming, and in this book, you'll learn why that happens so that you can work skillfully with your anxiety (even if your anxiety is painful or disruptive right now) and access its many gifts.

HOW I LEARNED TO EMBRACE ANXIETY

This book is a part of my years-long and sincere apology to anxiety. I didn't understand it well enough to include it in my 2010 book, *The Language of Emotions*, where I gave every other emotion *except* anxiety its own chapter. That was clueless of me, but now I know why: unlike people who feel anxiety intensely, I feel and respond to anxiety when it is very subtle (you may, too), so I saw it as a problem (that other people had) instead of an emotion.

Note: Your experience of anxiety (and all emotions) may be different from mine, because you're unique. Your neurology, your upbringing, and your socialization about emotions all have a significant effect on how you feel and work with emotions today. Even though I've been studying emotions for decades, I misunderstood anxiety almost completely, because my anxiety and I have a unique relationship that didn't track with the way most people talk about anxiety.

I learned about anxiety (from a radio show, of all places; I'll tell you more about that in chapter 1) soon after *The Language of Emotions* was published, and I later created a section on the gifts of anxiety in my 2013 book, *The Art of Empathy*. Still, anxiety deserves better than that. In fact, it deserves its very own book, and I'm glad to be able to write this book for my friend anxiety, and for you.

I've been studying emotions, empathy, and human behavior throughout my life, and I developed an empathic and emotion-honoring approach to emotions called Dynamic Emotional Integration® (also known as DEI). In DEI, we treat all emotions as vital aspects of everything we do: thinking, deciding, relating, behaving, acting, loving, dreaming, and healing. We see emotions as dynamic and lively aspects of our basic cognition and functioning that are present (at varying levels of intensity) in every moment of the day and night. DEI helps us integrate our emotions within ourselves so that they can do their best work.

Because emotions are always present and always working to support us, we learn to work directly with them, and I developed a group of skills that I call the Empathic Mindfulness practices to intentionally access the intelligence inside the emotions. These practices access emotions that help us ground and focus ourselves, set clear and loving boundaries, soothe and replenish ourselves, work directly with intense emotional states, and change or update our behaviors with the help of the very things that create and support our behaviors in the first place: our emotions. You'll learn these emotion-honoring mindfulness practices in chapter 3.

DEI is also dynamic, because you and your emotions are dynamic. You feel and respond to your emotions differently than other people do, and your ability to work with emotions shifts and changes throughout your life. Your emotions also change depending on the situations you face; emotions are a dynamic system. Because of this, I update DEI regularly to include new and helpful concepts about empathy and emotions (such as the healing purpose of anxiety, *ahem*). I've trained people across the world as DEI trainers and consultants, and many of these DEI professionals have joined me in an informal online group called the Anxioneers. We meet to laugh and connect and to create new ways to understand and work with anxiety.

I invited many of the Anxioneers to the group, because they are what I call *anxiety shrines*, or living sacred spaces where anxiety loves to visit. Isn't that a nice way to talk about someone who would otherwise be called anxiety disordered? In DEI, we don't ignore emotional disorders, but we do a great deal of reframing so that people can carry their specific emotional intensities with a sense of grace, humor, and possibilities. Certainly, we support therapeutic interventions when needed, yet we also know through decades of practice that many intense emotions will be able to contribute their gifts when people learn how to integrate them and work with them empathically and lovingly.

BRINGING EMPATHY TO YOUR EMOTIONS

What does it mean to work empathically with emotions? My definition of *empathy* is somewhat different from standard definitions (though there is not yet a single agreed-upon definition). Various philosophers and researchers define empathy as the capacity to feel

4

for and with other people, but I see empathy as larger and more complex than that. I see empathy not simply as a human-to-human emotional behavior, but also as our capacity to feel and engage deeply with anything and everything: animals, nature, language, concepts, ideas, emotions, art, music, mathematics, physics, science, and the entire universe.[1] When I talk about working empathically with emotions, I mean engaging with them, communicating with them, befriending them, and understanding their purpose so that they and we can do our best work together. I created DEI to help you work directly and empathically with the genius in your emotions.

In DEI, we organize the seventeen basic emotions into four families to help people identify them:

1. The Anger Family (anger, apathy, guilt/shame, and hatred)

2. The Fear Family (fear, anxiety, confusion, envy, jealousy, and panic)

3. The Sadness Family (sadness, grief, depression, and the suicidal urge)

4. The Happiness Family (happiness, contentment, and joy)

In this book, we'll focus on anxiety and the Fear Family, but we'll also bring in some important players from the other families (such as anger, shame, depression, and happiness, among others) that will help you engage beautifully with your anxiety so that it can do its best work within your healthy and integrated emotional realm.

This book is written for adults, but the concepts are presented in simple ways that children as young as eight or nine can understand (with the help of an older reader). If you've got younger children, I've included an appendix on helping little ones learn to embrace and play with their anxiety.

In each of the chapters ahead, I'll focus on a specific aspect of anxiety — or on a specific emotion that has been mistakenly identified as anxiety — and I'll share skills and ideas to help you work with your emotions in new ways. In part I, I'll reframe anxiety, help you understand its place in your emotional realm, and teach you a number of simple practices to help you work with it. In part II, I'll explore how anxiety works with (or trips over) nine different emotions and help you empathically approach and work with all of them empathically and effectively.

In part III, we'll bring everything together and explore ways to care for yourself if your job or lifestyle require heightened anxiety, and what you can do to soothe and support yourself during anxious and uncertain times when your anxiety *should* be active. There are many situations where you truly need your anxiety to be present and accounted for! But if you're struggling with anxiety right now, know that you're in the right place.

If you need support, you can skip ahead to chapter 4 to learn the specific DEI anxiety practice called Conscious Questioning for Anxiety. Anxiety is a wonderful and helpful emotion, but its dynamic focus and often-intense energy can destabilize you if you haven't learned anxiety-specific skills. In this book, you'll learn how to work with, listen to, empathize with, and befriend your anxiety so that it can help you get things done *without* disrupting your focus, your attention, your sleep, or your life unnecessarily.

WELCOMING YOUR ANXIETY

Your anxiety is a brilliant and vigilant emotion that looks ahead and helps you prepare for the future. Anxiety helps you identify problems and opportunities, and it brings you the energy and focus you need to face them. Anxiety also helps you complete your tasks and projects, and it gives you the push you need to meet your deadlines. But you wouldn't know any of that if you looked at most books on anxiety or listened to people complain about it. In most (or all?) cases, anxiety is treated as a problem: something to shut down, rationalize away, or get rid of. That's an unhelpful idea because anxiety is essential to pretty much everything you do.

Anxiety is also confused with other emotions (such as fear, panic, confusion, or shame), mostly because we're not taught to value our emotions or identify them clearly — which means that most of us don't learn how to recognize anxiety or work with it skillfully. In this book, we'll learn how to identify anxiety clearly and integrate it with its fellow emotions so that it will have the help it needs to do its best work.

I've designed this book in an anxiety-supportive way for busy people who may not have long stretches of time to sit and read. Each chapter is as compact and concise as I could make it, and each is divided into many short sections so that you can read up to a natural break and feel a sense of completion even if you don't have time to finish a chapter. You and your anxiety have a lot to do, and I want this book to support both of you. If you like, you can start an anxiety journal as you read this book. You can track the situations that increase or scramble your anxiety and contrast them with the situations that your anxiety already handles very well.

In the chapters ahead, you'll learn how to differentiate anxiety from *fear* (which helps you focus on the present moment); from *panic* (which is a lifesaving emotion that helps you fight, flee, or freeze when you need to); from *confusion* (which helps you take a break from focus when you need a rest); from *anger* (which helps you set clear boundaries around what you value); from *shame* (which helps you live up to your moral agreements); and from *depression* (which stops you from moving forward when something in your life simply cannot work). You'll also learn to work with your Happiness Family (happiness, contentment, and joy) so that they won't load you up with a thousand delightful ideas and tasks that no one's anxiety could possibly organize or complete.

You'll learn to treat anxiety as an essential part of your emotional realm and your ability to get things done. When your anxiety is welcomed and well situated in your psyche, it will contribute gifts and wisdom that are irreplaceable and that you'll fall in love with. *Really!*

Welcome to *Embracing Anxiety.*

PART I

Reframing
ANXIETY

1

Embracing the Foresight
and Focus of Anxiety

O ne of the biggest hurdles people face as they learn how to
work with anxiety is that they may not actually know what
anxiety is. As I did my research for *Embracing Anxiety*, I looked at
many other books on anxiety and saw it described in the following
ways (as well as others): intense energy; sweaty palms; muscular
tension, increased heart rate or adrenaline; dread; confusion or
blankness; a gnawing sense of impending failure or doom; feeling
frozen and on fire at the same time; or needing to escape. Sadly,
these authors are just as confused about anxiety as I was when I
wrote *The Language of Emotions* because what they're describing is
panic. Panic is a marvelous and lifesaving emotion that gives you
the energy you need to fight, flee, or freeze when your life is in
danger, but it's not anxiety.[1]

We'll explore panic in chapters 5 and 6 and discover supportive
ways to work with it, because it's a crucial (and intense) emotion.

In this chapter, however, we'll gently move panic aside and focus on anxiety so that you'll know what it is — and what it isn't.

Another issue is that many people mistakenly confuse the *emotion* of anxiety with mental health conditions such as generalized anxiety disorder, social anxiety, obsessive-compulsive disorder, panic attacks, and numerous phobias. These conditions do *contain* anxiety — along with other emotions, psychological distress, traumatic situations, or neurological conditions — but they're not *caused by* anxiety. Focusing only on the trouble we can get into with our emotions means that we may learn to see our emotions as problems instead of what they truly are: essential parts of our intelligence and our cognition, each of which brings us gifts, skills, and forms of genius that are irreplaceable.

I will lightly explore some of the mental health conditions that include anxiety, but I won't focus on them because this book is about embracing anxiety as a vital emotion that helps us get things done. If you're currently dealing with mental health conditions that hyperactivate (or suppress) your anxiety or panic, please work with your health-care team to address the situations that are destabilizing these powerful emotions. If you don't know where to start, there's a wonderful nonprofit website called HelpGuide (helpguide.org) that offers supportive and nonalarmist information on all aspects of mental health.[2] It's a great place to find clarity about what you're experiencing and what your next steps can be.

If you've mistakenly confused anxiety with other emotions, or with mental health conditions, you're not alone. Certainly, the authors of the books I read on anxiety confused it with panic or anxiety disorders, but my confusion wasn't any better than theirs. I knew that anxiety wasn't panic or fear because I could identify those emotions easily; fear contains our instincts and intuition about the present moment, and panic is the emotion that arises in endangering situations to save our lives. However, because I rarely felt what other people described as anxiety, I didn't identify it as a true emotion. I mistakenly treated anxiety as a problem that *other people* had because, to me, anxiety looked like a situation of poor emotion regulation rather than an emotion in its own right. It wasn't until late 2010, when I heard Dr. Mary Lamia on the radio, that I realized what had caused my emotional ignorance about anxiety.

Dr. Lamia is a clinical psychologist and educator who practices and teaches in the San Francisco Bay Area. She was on KQED's *Forum* program with host Michael Krasny to talk about her children's book *Understanding Myself: A Kid's Guide to Intense Emotions and Strong Feelings.*[3] I truly enjoyed listening to her because she treats emotions as aspects of intelligence and cognition. This is rare, and it was wonderful to hear about a children's book I could suggest to my readers. Toward the end of the interview when a caller asked about anxiety, Dr. Lamia talked about anxiety as the emotion that motivates us to get things done (such as tasks, plans, and projects big and small). She also noted that we respond to our anxiety in one of two ways. In one anxiety response, *procrastination*, people focus on deadlines and wait until their anxiety reaches a level of intensity that compels them to act, akin to leaping into a lake in one big jump. In the other anxiety response, *do-it-aheading*, people focus on individual tasks and complete them one after another on their way to a deadline, like carefully crossing a stream from stone to stone on their way to the lake.

As an example, if a task-focused do-it-aheader were planning a meeting, they would separate each of their preparations into small tasks, likely with a to-do list that prioritizes which tasks they should do first (reserve the room, send the invitations, organize the agenda, and so on). In contrast, a deadline-focused procrastinator might approach the meeting in a more big-picture way and perhaps set the date and the participant list first and then (seemingly) do very little until right before the meeting starts. We've all been taught that task-focused behavior is correct and organized, while procrastination is a sign of laziness, but Dr. Lamia strongly disagrees, and she's right. I've known many procrastinators who regularly complete masterful projects at the last minute, but like most of us, I was taught to see their accomplishments as luck instead of to understand that they work with their anxiety in a different way than I do.

I am a task-focused do-it-aheader. I rarely feel the intense anxiety that procrastinators do because I always respond to my anxiety when it's very subtle, and I complete many small tasks continually. This explains my ignorance about the more intense levels of anxiety that procrastinators feel and work with (often brilliantly). As a task-focused person, I manage my anxiety quite differently than deadline-focused people do. If I ever feel intense anxiety (I almost never do), it means that something has gone wrong: I've forgotten a task, fooled around, wasted my time, and failed (in the way I work with anxiety). For me, intense or obvious feelings of anxiety signal a serious problem.

For a deadline-focused procrastinator, on the other hand, intense feelings of anxiety can be normal and supportive. Dr. Lamia noted that a procrastinator can almost relax on her way to a deadline, secure in the knowledge that she will definitely complete her project, even if she has to drop everything else for hours or days in order to do so. A deadline-focused person's anxiety works in the background, nearly imperceptibly until the deadline looms, and then it springs into action, *shazam!* In contrast, a task-focused person's anxiety is more in the foreground, yet it may work at very subtle levels of activation as the person moves from task to task at a regular and consistent pace. What I have noticed as a task-focused person is that I work with subtle anxiety regularly throughout every day (for me, it's like a quiet voice continually asking, *Is this done? Does this need attention? What about this?*), while my deadline-focused friends experience anxiety as more of an intense special event (they might feel a powerful surge of anxiety close to the deadline and pull everything together in genius ways at the last minute).

Dr. Lamia notes that task-focused people with their moment-by-moment organizational skill get most of the praise, while deadline-focused people get most of the criticism — even though both anxiety styles have their genius and their downsides. Since 2010, I've explored anxiety empathically with the help of Dr. Lamia's concepts, and I've studied my own task-focused style and experimented with procrastination (I can *do* it, but I've never become truly comfortable with putting things off until a deadline looms).[4] I'm envious of successful procrastinators, and I've seen the downfalls of my task-focused style — but even though I've become more comfortable with procrastination (in manageable amounts), I will likely always be a task-focused person.[5] That's just how my anxiety works.

HOW YOUR ANXIETY WORKS

Your anxiety provides the essential support you need to think and plan, focus on the future, complete your tasks, and meet your deadlines. In fact, you couldn't get anything done without your anxiety. However, anxiety can also provide a great deal of energy, especially when a deadline is looming and you need to complete your project *now*. Anxiety can also ramp up its intensity when your neatly organized tasks get messed up by a bunch of new and disconnected tasks that won't line up in any kind of order.

Your anxiety may also be far-reaching, as you plan for your retirement over decades, for instance, or as you consider how your parenting today will affect your children later in life. Because anxiety is often focused on the future (on things that haven't happened yet), it can by its very nature be destabilizing. Your body lives in the present moment; it can remember the past and imagine the future, but it lives in the present. If you want to "be here now," all you need to do is focus on your body, *voila!*

But there are many situations in the past and the future that do need your attention, and anxiety and your other emotions will help you focus on and address them. Anxiety lives in the future, scanning possible situations, cataloging and prioritizing your tasks and deadlines, and recruiting skills, support, and your other emotions to help you arrive in the future prepared, on task, and effective. Anxiety also reaches back to your past to examine your resources, memories, ideas, mistakes, and failures so that you can move into the future in a way that will be efficient, appropriate for you, and as successful as possible. Anxiety can motivate you, disrupt you, energize you, focus you, or confuse you in its push to get things done well and on time.

One of the most supportive things you can do for anxiety is quite simple: make a list of everything you need to do, and cross tasks off your list regularly. List making leans into the gifts and skills of anxiety, and it can help you organize on paper (or on your computer, phone, or tablet) all of the information, competing threads, concerns, and ideas that anxiety brings up. Writing things down can clear space in your memory and help your anxiety soften because it knows that you're on the job, that it's not alone, and that you're listening.

Of course, *how* you organize your lists is important because, as you may have found, unfocused lists may confuse or overwhelm you and your anxiety. It's also important to know whether you're a task-focused person or a deadline-focused person so that your lists can support the way you work best. (I'll share some specific list-making ideas to support you and your anxiety in chapter 4.) And it's important to realize that far-reaching projects such as child rearing or planning for retirement will require not just lists, but research, long-term planning (with space for change and flexibility over time), input, and a supportive community. Your lists and plans can help your anxiety relax, but you also need lots of information and social support to complete complex and long-range projects.

Anxiety is a vigilant, resourceful, and tireless emotion that does *a lot* for you. But because it can be so activating and future focused, it can feel uncomfortable or even overwhelming. Later, I'll share practices for anxiety that will help you ground and focus yourself, gather all of the energy and information you need, make focused lists, and work gracefully with your anxiety (instead of work against it). In this chapter, I want you to identify anxiety clearly so that you won't mistake it for panic, fear, confusion, or any other emotion. Anxiety has a unique job as an individual emotion, but it also has an important function within your emotional system as a whole.

HOW YOUR ANXIETY ENGAGES WITH YOUR OTHER EMOTIONS

Emotions bring you gifts and skills that help you think, decide, act, love, dream, and heal. Each of your emotions contributes specific abilities that help you make sense of your world and act as skillfully as you can in each situation. They take care of you, they protect you, and they support you. Your emotions work together, often in pairs or groups, to help you meet whichever situations you encounter. Something that can confuse you (if you don't know that your emotions *should* work together) is that many anxiety-provoking situations can activate other emotions alongside anxiety.

For instance, if you're postponing things, and you aren't listening carefully to your anxiety, your guilt and shame may arise. The presence of these emotions is normal and necessary, and when your guilt and shame are well integrated in your emotional life, they'll help you live up to your agreements and your ethics. Your guilt and shame will also warn you when you offend someone or let yourself or others down (or are about to). When you're delaying your work past a reasonable point (or avoiding your tasks), your guilt and shame may arise to help you complete your work. But as you may have experienced, anxiety that arises in combination with guilt and shame can be difficult to tolerate: these emotions can be insistent, nagging, or even overwhelming! When your intense emotions work together like this, your emotional skills (or lack of skills) can be the difference between comfort and misery, or between success and failure.

Your anxiety may team up with any of your other emotions, depending on your situation, your emotional awareness, your physical condition, and your needs. For instance, your anxiety can pair up with your anger, which helps you set boundaries and lets you know what's important to you. If you've got emotional skills, you'll be able to identify both emotions and work with them in turn: you'll be able to set clear and loving boundaries with the help of your anger, and you'll be able to prepare yourself, gather your resources, and complete your tasks with the help of your anxiety.

But if you don't have strong emotional skills, you might lash out at people and set harsh or painful boundaries with your anger, or you might repress your anger and refuse to set any boundaries at all. You might also feel destabilized by your anxiety and try to run away from it or shut it down in any way you can. When you don't have the skills that you need to work with your emotions, they can feel miserable, irrational, or out of control.

But if you can welcome your emotions as vital parts of your intelligence and know that they're always trying to help you and bring you specific skills, then you can shift your attitude and pay loving attention to them. When you can work with your emotions as your friends and allies, even when they're intense, you can change every part of your life and discover the emotional genius that has been working inside you your entire life.

One of the genius aspects of anxiety is that it scans your interior life and your emotional health in order to assess your readiness for upcoming tasks and challenges. This is something that Anxioneer Jennifer Nate from Alberta, Canada, discovered in her work as a DEI trainer and consultant, and as a DEI instructor online. Jen and fellow Anxioneer Sarah Alexander from Oregon (who is a DEI professional and a licensed clinical social worker) have helped the rest of us observe anxiety working not just to complete our exterior tasks, but also to complete our interior tasks. We began to see that anxiety helps us attend to the depression we're ignoring, feel the sadness or grief we push aside, work with the traumatic memories that affect our current decisions, or make amends for something we've done wrong, and so forth. This may be one of the reasons that anxiety is mistaken for panic and other emotions; our anxiety may be focusing our attention on suppressed emotions or painful experiences because allowing them to fester or be ignored is inefficient and will likely reduce our effectiveness in the future. Jen and Sarah helped us understand the interior task-completion function of anxiety, and this created an entirely new level of understanding in our Anxioneers community.

ANXIETY AND YOUR SOCIAL INSIGHT

Anxiety also works to help you understand and maintain your place in social groups. Though it is generally hidden from your everyday awareness, you have many different behaviors and personas that you can access based on where you are and who you're with. A simple example is contrasting who you are and how you behave when you're at home in your pajamas with who you are and how you behave when you're dressed up and "on" at work or school. Your social behavior and insight rely on anxiety (and other emotions) because you need to think about how your current behavior is going to play out in the future. It is not only tasks and deadlines that live in the future; a projected part of your current self does, too, and it is in your best interest to arrive in that future as prepared as you can be.

Your anxiety (with the help of your fear and other emotions) scans your social environment and prepares you to interact in ways that will be appropriate and effective. If you're in an unfamiliar social situation, your feelings of anxiety may increase in order to help you pilot your way through the novel situation. If you think back to a time when you came upon a social group that felt unusual to you — because of differences in age, culture, occupation, class, gender, or behavior — you may have noticed that your anxiety increased (along with many other emotions). In these situations, anxiety has an important task: it prepares you for the unknown, scans your memories for relevant social information, studies the group to figure out the norms, and helps you increase your awareness. You may have experienced this as nervousness, shyness, or stage fright, but it was likely anxiety helping you read the room and figure out which of your many behaviors and personas would work best.

This social insight and the work you do to shift your behavior in different social groups is extremely valuable; you couldn't get by without it. However, it is *work*, and it's work that tends to be more constant or more required if you are in a lower social position (for instance, if you're an employee interacting with a manager or a boss, a student interacting with a teacher or dean, a child interacting with an adult, and so forth). When you're in a subordinate position, your anxiety may need to be activated regularly so that you can choose the behaviors that will help you succeed in your unequal social group. This activation is also necessary if you're a member of a marginalized group that has been identified as less valuable or that has been exiled from the allegedly normal world (for instance, people of color, LGBTQIA+ people, disabled people, women, elders, youth, people of varying body weights and sizes, and so forth). If you're outside the tiny sliver of behavior that is alleged to be normal (especially if your differences are visible), your anxiety may need to be on constant alert and may require the support of fear (and possibly panic; see chapter 5) to help you navigate through an unwelcoming or even perilous social world. And of course, if you're in an abusive relationship, your anxiety and panic will need to be on the job all day and all night.

Here in the United States, it has long been known that people who are the targets of discrimination and exclusion often deal with anxiety disorders, panic disorders, depression, and poor health outcomes because their bodies and their emotions are on high alert for much of their lives. Emotions contain a lot of necessary energy, and that's wonderful. But it can also be troublesome if your emotions need to be highly activated and vigilant (for whatever reason) most of the time. As we study our friend anxiety and learn to embrace its genius, we'll explore ways to reframe our responses to it when it needs to work at intense levels of activation.

As you learn to observe and work with anxiety as a valuable member of your social skills and your emotional realm — even when it needs to be on high alert — it will help to know about four ideas that can make all the difference in your emotional life.

THE FOUR KEYS TO EMOTIONAL GENIUS

First things first: Most of us have received a very poor emotional education. Most of us don't know how emotions work or why, we don't have a large emotional vocabulary, and we've been taught to see many emotions as unwanted, unlovable, or unmanageable — which means that we can't embrace those emotions or listen to them clearly. Emotions have, throughout the centuries, been treated as *less than*: less than spirituality, less than the intellect, less than scientific inquiry, and less than good old common sense. Emotions are often seen as irrational, embarrassing, or unnecessary things.

Even in fields where emotions should be a main focus, such as psychiatry, psychology, and neurology, emotions are often treated as problems or afterthoughts or as much less important than the so-called rational processes. Thankfully, this is slowly changing.

In *The Language of Emotions*, I write a great deal about the centuries of emotion-trashing ideas we humans have been subjected to (and still are subjected to). While that long, sad history is interesting, my friend anxiety suggests that I can speed things up in this book and focus on helping you work with emotions in new ways.

As I've studied our backward and unhelpful emotional education, I've identified four key concepts that can help you see and experience your emotions as supportive parts of your awareness, your social skills, your empathy, and your intelligence.

1. There are no negative emotions, and there are no positive emotions, either.

All emotions are messengers that tell you how you're feeling and what's going on. Each of your emotions has important messages for you, and all of them bring you the skills, awareness, and energy you need in every situation. Even though the way you work with your emotions can have positive or negative outcomes, your emotions themselves are not good or bad.

Unfortunately, the idea that emotions are positive or negative is promoted in most of psychology, psychiatry, and neurology, where emotions are sorted into positive and negative categories, or *valences*.[6] In DEI, we *unvalence* the emotions immediately because if you think of emotions as good or bad (wanted or unwanted, pro-social or antisocial, and so on), you'll create a problem inside yourself almost immediately.

Here's why: If you think that an emotion is positive, yet you rarely feel it, what might you feel instead? Likely you'll feel shame, anger, grief, confusion, anxiety, and so on. And now, instead of being able focus on that original emotion, you'll have to deal with an emotion pile-up that may be confusing or painful to experience. You might also chase after that supposedly positive emotion and try to feel it no matter what's going on in your life.

The same situation occurs when you think that an emotion is negative. If I tell you that an emotion is negative, yet you usually feel it, you might also feel anger, fear, sadness, depression, and so on. Once again, you won't be able to focus on the original emotion because so many other emotions have been called to the scene. The idea that emotions are negative or positive absolutely interferes with your basic emotional functioning, and it's the first emotion concept we challenge in DEI. Valencing teaches us to chase after certain emotions as if they're prizes and avoid other emotions as if they're diseases or character flaws. Valencing emotions can stop us from developing a full range of emotional skills.

All emotions bring you intelligence and information, and all of them can help you understand what's happening inside you and in your world. All emotions are necessary, and all of them deserve to be welcomed, befriended, listened to, and treated with respect. This is especially important when you're learning to work with an emotion like anxiety, which has been flung into the negative category. Seeing your anxiety instead as valuable and necessary (rather than negative *or* positive) will help you respond to it perceptively so that you can develop a healthy and workable relationship with it.

2. Emotions arise at many different levels of intensity, and vocabulary is essential.

The second important key to understanding and working well with your emotions — especially the ones that have been mistakenly identified as negative — is to expand your emotional vocabulary. It's vital to learn how to identify your emotions at every level of intensity, and there is a wonderful benefit to increasing your emotional awareness and vocabulary. Researcher Lisa Feldman Barrett and her colleagues have found that simply developing a larger emotional vocabulary helps you develop stronger emotion-regulation skills.[7] This research suggests that if you can name your emotions with precision, you can calm your entire body and help yourself organize everything you're feeling.

Your emotions are always present; they're not momentary moods or attitudes. They're important parts of your ability to think, feel, decide, behave, and act, and they're always watching out for you. But people tend not to be aware of emotions unless they're obvious. Some emotions can arise in such a soft state that you and others might not even notice that they're there. As I mentioned, my anxiety regularly arose in a subtle way, as an inner voice that gently reminded me about my tasks: *Did you complete this chore? Do you know where that part of the project is?* I didn't realize this was anxiety, but thankfully, I've learned how to identify my subtle anxiety and work with it intentionally. Some of the vocabulary words I use to describe my soft levels of anxiety today are *careful, attentive, aware, watchful, anticipatory, prepared,* or *organized.*

Your emotions can also arise in a more noticeable state, where you can more easily feel them and name them. At this more obvious level of intensity, you would know if an emotion was, for instance, happiness, sadness, anger, or anxiety. Some vocabulary words for a medium level of anxiety might be *alert, apprehensive, disconcerted, uneasy, anxious, unsettled,* or *nervous.*

In some situations, your emotions can arise in an intense state, where they're very noticeable to you and the people around you. At this intense level, your emotion-regulation skills will be the key to maintaining your focus so that you don't lose your way and destabilize yourself or others. Some vocabulary words for an intense level of anxiety might be *tense, overwhelmed, jumpy, rattled, flustered,* or *alarmed.*

Many people can only identify anxiety when it reaches this intense level. This can be a problem because if they don't know how to identify subtle and medium levels of anxiety, or how to regulate intense anxiety, they may mistakenly see anxiety as an always-intense emotion that always causes trouble. A big reason that people valence certain emotions as negative is that they haven't learned what the emotion does, how it works, or how to identify it when it's soft and subtle.

Your emotional vocabulary and your ability to identify your emotions is especially important in regard to anxiety because the increase in intensity that many people feel when they're deeply anxious can be overwhelming or frightening. It can even feel as if you're having a heart attack (women take note, however; heart attacks can feel like anxiety for us).[8] Self-soothing, steady breathing, and calming practices can help when your anxiety is intense (which usually means that panic is in the mix; see chapter 6), but so can naming your level of anxiety with precision. Dr. Barrett's research suggests that helping your body understand that you're feeling anxiety (and not experiencing a serious illness) can ease or halt the domino effect of increased worry, fear, panic, and overwhelm.

If your anxiety is subtle, your vocabulary will help you learn how to identify and work with it. And if your anxiety is intense, your vocabulary will help you calm and soothe yourself. When you have a larger anxiety vocabulary, you can also learn how to track the arc of your anxiety and to work with it as skillfully at softer levels as you do when it is insistent and noticeable.

In the next chapter, I've included the DEI Emotional Vocabulary Lists, which are organized by emotion category and level of emotional activation, to help you increase your ability to identify and work with your emotions at every level of intensity.

3. It is normal for emotions to work in pairs, groups, and clusters.

We usually learn about emotions as single events: We can be happy *or* sad, but not both; we can feel contented but not envious; or if we feel any emotion alongside anger, anger becomes a secondhand emotion. This is an idea that most of us have learned, but it's wrong, and it creates emotional ignorance.

It is absolutely normal to feel more than one emotion at the same time. When you understand emotions as aspects of your basic intelligence and cognition, then it makes sense that you would often need more than one emotion working to support you. Vocabulary here (at least in English) is a huge stumbling block that keeps so many of us unaware of the normal behavior of emotions. Though it is ordinary and necessary for multiple emotions to arise at the same time, there are only four words in the English language that describe multiple emotions. Four! They are *bittersweet*, which describes feeling happiness (or joy) and sadness (or grief) at the same time; *gloating*, which describes an angry kind of intense joy about winning at the expense of a person who has lost (gloating also involves shaming the loser); *nostalgic*, which is a current sadness (or grief) about a past happiness (or joy); and *ambivalent*, the definition of which highlights the problems of both inadequate vocabulary and valencing, *as if there is such a thing as opposing emotions — it's absurd!*

If you look back at the first key to emotional genius, you'll see that we're working to *unvalence* the emotions and get rid of the simplistic positive and negative valencing that make us so emotionally confused. The word *ambivalent* means *both valences*, and it suggests that if you feel one positive emotion and one negative emotion at the same time, you'll become confused and unable to make a decision. The word *ambivalence* tells us that feeling two emotions at once will essentially immobilize us! English language, *what?*

Vocabulary is so important in helping us understand concepts, yet English fails us in regard to multiple emotions because it doesn't contain enough words to help us understand how emotions truly work. In DEI, we play around and create new blended emotion words so that we won't be impeded by the severe lack in our English vocabulary. Throughout this book, I'll share some of our made-up emotion words, such as *panger* (panic and anger), *panxiety* (panic and anxiety), *jealenvy* (jealousy and envy), *shangrief* (shame, anger, and grief), and so on. Our deeply limited English language can't stop us from understanding how emotions work!

Understanding that emotions *should* work together is especially important in your work with anxiety because anxiety often needs the support of other emotions, such as fear, confusion, shame, contentment, anger, panic, and so on. This is a healthy thing, and it's different from reacting to your supposedly "negative" emotions and creating an unnecessary emotion pile-up. In many situations, your anxiety needs assistance from its fellow emotions. When you're focused on a job or a deadline is looming, your anxiety may need the support of other emotions to help you do your best work. We'll explore these emotional pairings throughout this book, and as you learn to identify and befriend your emotions, you won't be thrown when they show up together. When your emotions are your friends, they won't feel like a pile-up. In fact, you may welcome them all because they each contain a unique form of genius. The more the merrier!

4. Learn how to channel your emotions skillfully and appropriately.

Many of us have only two options when an emotion (or a group of emotions) arises: we can express them outwardly or repress them inwardly. Expression and repression can take many forms, but they have one thing in common: both responses tend to throw the energy of emotions away.

Let's look at the expression and repression of anger, which helps you set boundaries around what's important to you and relay that information to others. If you *express* your anger outward through harsh words or physical movements, you may set a boundary, but it may disturb or break the boundaries of others. The targets of your expressed anger may understand your boundary and what's important to you, but they may also feel distrustful, fearful, or hurt. Throwing your anger outward can create trouble or pain for you and others, and it can damage your relationships, which is the exact opposite of what anger should do.

If you *repress* your anger instead, you'll erase your ability to recognize what's important or set a clear boundary, and other people may not know where your boundaries are or what you need. If those people are loving and caring, they'll find a way to learn about you and relate to you, but it will be *work* for them because you're not sending clear signals. If people are uncaring, or don't have time to figure out what you need, they may trample over the boundaries you don't know how to set and ignore things that are important to you.

With anxiety, if you *express* it outward, you may run yourself ragged as you complete every task and project but forget to eat, sleep, or take care of things that are not related to your work. You may become a kind of anxiety android who is pushed around by anxiety, and you won't be in the driver's seat of your life. Anxiety — like every other emotion — should be your partner and friend, not your taskmaster.

However, if you *repress* your anxiety and refuse to complete your tasks or plan for your future (because it's too hard, or you don't have what you need, or your focus is poor, and so on), of course you won't get things done. But because anxiety is such an essential part of your basic functioning, repressing it will only make it come at you with more intensity. Repressing anxiety might seem like a good self-care practice in the moment, but anxiety is necessary, and repression will initiate emotional turmoil as your anxiety attempts to reassert itself. I've seen this turmoil lead people into addictions and distractions of all kinds, including obsessive exercise or obsessive meditation. It takes *a lot* of energy to repress an energetic emotion like anxiety.

But let me be clear: expression and repression are healthy responses in many situations. For instance, if you feel a lot of sadness, and it's safe to cry, it's great to express your sadness and your tears so that you can let go. But if it's not safe to cry, and you understand sadness, you can soften your body, breathe in quietly, and let go as you exhale. You can repress your tears and sadness on the outside but still honor your sadness in the privacy of your own body.

If you don't understand sadness, however, your repression may be a way to pretend that you don't feel it. This kind of repression may train you to see your unwanted and unloved sadness as an obstacle or a sign of weakness (and that's truly sad). Expression and repression have their place, but if you *only* express your emotions outwardly or repress them inwardly as if they are problems, you (and the people you love) may learn to see all emotions as trouble. This is especially true when you're dealing with intense emotions and multiple emotions.

Luckily, there is a healthy middle path between expression and repression, which I call *channeling*. Channeling your emotions is an empathic engagement process that helps you learn what your emotions do and how they work so that you can work with them mindfully and intentionally. Channeling means listening to your emotions and working with their unique gifts so that they can contribute their intelligence and energy to you and then recede gracefully.

For instance, to channel your sadness, you would know that your sadness helps you let go of things that aren't working anymore, and you would use your sadness to let go of things mindfully (including ideas, attitudes, physical tension, or old, tired ways of working with emotions). When you can let go, your sadness will recede to a softer, almost imperceptible intensity until it's time to let go of things again. Or to channel your anger, you would know that anger helps you set boundaries and state what's important, so you would use its gifts to find your certainty and your focused and assertive voice. When you can set your boundaries skillfully and state what's true for you without harming others, your anger will also recede to a softer and almost imperceptible level of intensity until you need it to set a boundary again.

Channeling is a healing approach to any emotion, but in the territory of anxiety, it can be life changing. When you can identify your anxiety as the emotion that helps you complete your tasks and meet your deadlines, your approach to it can become mindful, loving, and effective. To channel your anxiety, you would know that it is trying to help you prepare, so you would work in partnership with your anxiety to work smarter, look ahead for deadlines and possible problems, create focused lists, and look behind and inside yourself for possible obstacles. Channeling can help you work *with* your anxiety instead of being worked over by it. Channeling can help you approach your emotions as important parts of your intelligence, your awareness, your social skills, and your ability to get things done.

BRINGING THE FOUR KEYS TOGETHER

When you can unvalence your emotions, develop your emotional vocabulary, and channel single and multiple emotions skillfully, you'll be able to embrace all of them and learn their unique language. Your integrated emotional skills will help you in every area of your life, and they'll be especially helpful as you learn how to support your hardworking anxiety.

Anxiety often increases in intensity as your tasks increase or your deadlines approach, and the Emotional Vocabulary Lists in the next chapter will help you identify and organize your anxious sensations so that you can acclimate to the situation. Your anxiety may also recruit other emotions to help with your tasks and deadlines — and your ability to treat multiple emotions as completely normal will help you remain focused and effective. Also, accepting your anxiety as necessary and normal instead of positive or negative will help you welcome it instead of reacting to it and adding more activation to your already-activated system. When you can reframe your anxiety with these four keys, you'll find that channeling your anxiety and helping it help you will become easier.

In the next chapter, I'll introduce you to anxiety and its friends: the seventeen emotions that will help you think, decide, feel, act, and live more intentionally. When you know how to identify your emotions and work with them as your friends and partners, you'll have access to clearer self-awareness, better understanding of others, and more options in every area of your life. Also, you and your anxiety will have their support so that you can do your best work together.

2

Meeting Your
Four Emotion Families

Your emotions are important messengers that tell you how you're feeling and what's going on — inside and outside of you — and they work to support you in every moment of every day. Each of your emotions is essential, and all of them bring you the skills, energy, and intelligence you need in each situation you encounter. For instance, as we've learned so far, anxiety helps you complete your tasks and meet your deadlines, anger helps you set boundaries around what's important, and sadness helps you let go of things that aren't working any longer. All emotions have specific functions, and all of them contain unique gifts, skills, and intelligence.

Though each of us has unique emotional experiences — based on our upbringing, our temperament, our emotional training, and our individual responses — I was able to organize emotions into categories by focusing on what they do. Instead of focusing on facial expressions or bodily sensations, which are not shared or reliable ways to identify emotions, I focused on how we understand and use emotions. I studied each emotion in relation to what was happening, how people responded, and what they did with the emotion in question.

Some emotions, such as anger, were easy to organize because their purpose is so obvious: for instance, anger helps people set boundaries around what they value. *How* people set those boundaries — with clarity, weakness, or violence — was completely dependent on their emotional skills (or lack of skills), but the *purpose* of anger remains stable in all cases.

Some emotions, such as anxiety, were harder to figure out, either because I didn't feel them in stereotypical ways, or because the emotions were so demonized that people repressed them or refused to admit to feeling them (think of jealousy, envy, hatred, and shame, among others). But every emotion eventually responded to my empathic inquiries (thank you, my friends!), and I was able to create the grand unified theory of emotions that became Dynamic Emotional Integration.

In DEI, we work to make the emotions as easy to understand as possible without simplifying them too much. We've found that organizing the emotions into four families helps people identify and empathize with them more easily. The short lists that follow present the seventeen emotions, the gifts they bring you, and the empathic questions you can ask them that will help you understand and work with them as your friends and guides.

Because this book focuses on anxiety, I won't be covering all seventeen emotions in detail. In later chapters, I'll focus on nine emotions that will help you work with your anxiety, but I've included all of the emotions in this chapter so that you can see them in one place. If you'd like more detailed information about specific emotions, see the notes for this chapter.[1]

The four basic emotion families are the Anger Family, the Fear Family, the Sadness Family, and the Happiness Family. Each emotion family contains a specific kind of intelligence that helps guide your thoughts and actions so that you can understand yourself and the world around you.

The emotion family tables that follow can help you understand what your emotions do, what gifts they bring you, and the questions you can ask to help you channel your emotions empathically and intentionally (instead of merely expressing or repressing them). Beneath each family table, I'm including the emotional vocabulary words I've gathered over the years, organized by family and intensity, and alphabetized (note the three levels of organization in these lists; my anxiety approves!). These lists are not exhaustive, but they're a good start. You may enjoy finding even more precise words for your unique emotions and sensations.

In this chapter, you'll meet the seventeen emotions as individuals within their families so that you can identify them more easily. When we get to part II, we'll focus on the relationships between anxiety and nine key emotions (fear, confusion, panic, anger, shame, depression, happiness, contentment, and joy) and learn about how they work together (or stumble over each other sometimes).

UNDERSTANDING THE ANGER FAMILY: BOUNDARIES, RULES, AND BEHAVIORS

The emotions in your Anger Family (anger, guilt/shame, apathy, and hatred) tell you what's important and when a boundary has been crossed or a rule has been broken. These emotions help you set behavioral guidelines for yourself and others.

When you set and maintain clear boundaries, you'll know where you begin and end, what's yours, what's important, and which behaviors you value. Your ability to set healthy boundaries and maintain healthy behaviors with your Anger Family will help you and your anxiety organize your life more easily.

Emotion	Gifts and Skills	Internal Questions
ANGER arises when your self-image, behaviors, values, or interpersonal boundaries are challenged — or when you see them challenged in someone else.	Honor, certainty, healthy self-esteem, proper boundaries, healthy detachment, protection of yourself and others	*What do I value?* *What must be protected and restored?*
APATHY (*or BOREDOM*) is a protective mask for anger, and it arises in situations where you are not able or willing to work with your anger openly.	Detachment, boundary setting, separation, taking a time-out	*What is being avoided?* *What must be made conscious?*
GUILT/SHAME arise to make sure that you don't hurt, embarrass, or dehumanize yourself or others.	Integrity, self-respect, making amends, behavioral guidelines, behavioral change	*Who has been hurt?* *What must be made right?*
HATRED arises in the presence of your shadow, or things you cannot accept in yourself (and despise in others). *Shadow work* can help you explore these things so that you can detoxify and reintegrate them and move toward wholeness.[2]	Intense awareness, sudden evolution, shadow work	*What has fallen into my shadow?* *What must be reintegrated?*

Emotional Vocabulary for the Anger Family

ANGER, APATHY, AND HATRED

SOFT ANGER AND APATHY

Annoyed • Apathetic • Bored • Certain • Cold • Crabby • Cranky • Critical • Cross • Detached • Displeased • Frustrated • Impatient • Indifferent • Irritated • Peeved • Rankled

MEDIUM ANGER

Affronted • Aggravated • Angry • Antagonized • Arrogant • Bristling • Exasperated • Incensed • Indignant • Inflamed • Mad • Offended • Resentful • Riled up • Sarcastic

INTENSE ANGER AND HATRED

Aggressive • Appalled • Belligerent • Bitter • Contemptuous • Disgusted • Furious • Hateful • Hostile • Irate • Livid • Menacing • Outraged • Ranting • Raving • Seething • Spiteful • Vengeful • Vicious • Vindictive • Violent

GUILT/SHAME

SOFT GUILT/SHAME

Abashed • Awkward • Discomfited • Flushed • Flustered • Hesitant • Humble • Reticent • Self-conscious • Speechless • Withdrawn

MEDIUM GUILT/SHAME

Ashamed • Chagrined • Contrite • Culpable • Embarrassed • Guilty • Humbled • Intimidated • Penitent • Regretful • Remorseful • Reproachful • Rueful • Sheepish

INTENSE GUILT/SHAME

Belittled • Degraded • Demeaned • Disgraced • Guilt-ridden • Guilt-stricken • Humiliated • Mortified • Ostracized • Self-condemning • Self-flagellating • Shamefaced • Stigmatized

UNDERSTANDING THE FEAR FAMILY: INSTINCTS, INTUITION, ORIENTING, AND ACTION

The emotions in your Fear Family (fear, anxiety, confusion, jealousy, envy, and panic) contain your intuition and your instincts. These emotions help you orient to your surroundings; notice change, novelty, or hazards; and take effective action. I'll highlight four of the emotions in the Fear Family in this book so that you'll understand their purpose and how each of them interacts with and supports your anxiety.

Emotion	Gifts and Skills	Internal Questions
FEAR arises to help you focus on **the present moment**, access your instincts and intuition, and tune in to changes in your immediate environment.	Intuition, instincts, focus, clarity, attentiveness, readiness	*What action should be taken?*
ANXIETY (*or WORRY*) is focused on **the future**. It arises to help you look ahead and identify the tasks you need to complete or the deadlines you need to meet.	Foresight, focus, task completion, procrastination alert!	*What brought this feeling forward?* *What **truly** needs to get done?*

Emotion	Gifts and Skills	Internal Questions
CONFUSION is a mask for fear and anxiety that arises when you have too much to process all at once. Confusion can give you a much-needed time-out.	Soft awareness, spaciness, flexibility, taking a time-out	*What is my intention?* *What action should be taken?*
PANIC arises when you face threats to your survival. Panic gives you three lifesaving choices: *fight, flee,* or *freeze.*	Sudden energy, intense attention, absolute stillness, survival	During an emergency: *Just listen to your body.* Fight, flee, or freeze. Your body is a survival expert, and it will keep you safe. For panic that relates to past difficulties or traumas: *What has been frozen in time?* *What healing action must be taken?*
JEALOUSY arises when your connection to love, loyalty, or security in your relationships is challenged.	Fairness, commitment, security, love, connection, loyalty	*What has been betrayed?* *What must be healed and restored?*
ENVY arises when your connection to material security, resources, or recognition is challenged.	Fairness, security, access to resources, proper recognition, self-preservation	*What has been betrayed?* *What must be made right?*

Emotional Vocabulary for the Fear Family

FEAR, ANXIETY, CONFUSION, AND PANIC

SOFT FEAR, ANXIETY, AND PANIC

Alert • Apprehensive • Cautious • Concerned • Confused •
Curious • Disconcerted • Disoriented • Disquieted •

Doubtful • Edgy • Energized • Fidgety • Hesitant • Indecisive • Insecure • Instinctive • Intuitive • Leery • Pensive • Shy • Timid • Uneasy • Watchful

MEDIUM FEAR, ANXIETY, AND PANIC

Afraid • Alarmed • Anxious • Aversive • Distrustful • Fearful • Jumpy • Nervous • Perturbed • Rattled • Shaky • Startled • Suspicious • Unnerved • Unsettled • Wary • Worried

INTENSE FEAR AND PANIC

Filled with Dread • Horrified • Panicked • Paralyzed • Petrified • Phobic • Shocked • Terrorized

JEALOUSY AND ENVY

SOFT JEALOUSY AND ENVY

Disbelieving • Distrustful • Insecure • Protective • Suspicious • Vulnerable

MEDIUM JEALOUSY AND ENVY

Covetous • Demanding • Desirous • Envious • Jealous • Threatened

INTENSE JEALOUSY AND ENVY

Avaricious • Gluttonous • Grasping • Greedy • Green with envy • Persistently jealous • Possessive • Resentful

UNDERSTANDING THE SADNESS FAMILY: STOPPING, LETTING GO, AND RECOVERING

The emotions in your Sadness Family (sadness, grief, situational depression, and the suicidal urge) help you release things that aren't working and mourn things that are gone so that you can relax, let go, and rejuvenate yourself. Learning to let go and learning to soothe and calm yourself with the emotions in your Sadness Family will help you and your anxiety clear out unimportant or outdated tasks and deadlines so that you can work efficiently and gracefully.

Emotion	Gifts and Skills	Internal Questions
SADNESS arises to help you let go of things that aren't working for you. If you can let go, you'll be able to relax, recover, and revitalize yourself.	Release, relaxation, rejuvenation	*What must be released?* *What must be rejuvenated?*
GRIEF arises when you have lost something — a person, an idea, a belief, a thing, or a situation — that you cannot get back.	Sorrow, remembrance, honoring of loss, deep release	*What must be mourned?* *What must be released completely?*
SITUATIONAL DEPRESSION arises when things are not working well, and you lose the energy to keep going in the ways you previously did. There's always an important reason for situational depression to arise.	The ingenious stop sign of the soul	*Where has my energy gone?* *Why was it sent away?*

Emotion	Gifts and Skills	Internal Questions
THE SUICIDAL URGE arises when something in your life needs to end — but not your actual, physical life! It's important to reach out for help and identify the situation or thing that needs to end so that you can get your life back.	Certainty, finality, freedom, transformation, rebirth	*What idea or behavior must end now?* *What can I no longer tolerate?* *Important:* If you're in crisis, please reach out to a counselor, doctor, loved one, or your local crisis hotline.[3]

Emotional Vocabulary for the Sadness Family

SADNESS, GRIEF, AND DEPRESSION

SOFT SADNESS

Contemplative • Disappointed • Disconnected • Distracted • Grounded • Listless • Low • Steady • Regretful • Wistful

MEDIUM SADNESS, GRIEF, AND DEPRESSION

Dejected • Discouraged • Dispirited • Down • Downtrodden • Drained • Forlorn • Gloomy • Grieving • Heavy-hearted • Melancholy • Mournful • Sad • Sorrowful • Weepy • World-weary

INTENSE SADNESS, GRIEF, AND DEPRESSION

Anguished • Bereaved • Bleak • Depressed • Despairing • Despondent • Grief-stricken • Heartbroken • Hopeless • Inconsolable • Morose

DEPRESSION AND SUICIDAL URGES

SOFT DEPRESSION AND SUICIDAL URGES

Apathetic • Constantly irritated, Angry (or Enraged; see the Anger vocabulary list on page 39) • Depressed • Discouraged • Disinterested • Dispirited • Feeling worthless • Flat • Helpless • Humorless • Impulsive • Indifferent • Isolated • Lethargic • Listless • Melancholy • Pessimistic • Purposeless • Withdrawn • World-weary

MEDIUM DEPRESSION AND SUICIDAL URGES

Bereft • Crushed • Desolate • Despairing • Desperate • Drained • Empty • Fatalistic • Hopeless • Joyless • Miserable • Morbid • Overwhelmed • Passionless • Pleasureless • Sullen

INTENSE SUICIDAL URGES

Agonized • Anguished • Bleak • Death-seeking • Devastated • Doomed • Gutted • Nihilistic • Numbed • Reckless • Self-destructive • Suicidal • Tormented • Tortured

Important: If you're in crisis, please reach out to a counselor, doctor, loved one, or your local crisis hotline.[4]

UNDERSTANDING THE HAPPINESS FAMILY: HOPE, CONFIDENCE, AND INSPIRATION

The emotions in your Happiness Family (happiness, contentment, and joy) help you look around you, at yourself, or toward the future with hope, satisfaction, and delight. Learning to work respectfully with your Happiness Family — and making sure that they don't say *yes!* to too many things — is a key to creating a life that your anxiety can manage.

Emotion	Gifts and Skills	Internal Statements
HAPPINESS arises to help you look around you and toward the future with hope and enjoyment.	Amusement, hope, delight, playfulness	*Thank you for this lively celebration!*
CONTENTMENT arises after you've accomplished a task, and it helps you look toward yourself with pride and satisfaction.	Satisfaction, self-esteem, confidence, healthy pride	*Thank you for renewing my faith in myself!*
JOY arises to help you feel a blissful sense of openhearted connection to others, to ideas, or to experiences.	Expansion, inspiration, brilliance, bliss	*Thank you for this wonderful moment!*

Emotional Vocabulary for the Happiness Family

HAPPINESS, CONTENTMENT, AND JOY

SOFT HAPPINESS

Amused • Calm • Encouraged • Friendly • Hopeful • Inspired • Jovial • Open • Peaceful • Smiling • Upbeat

MEDIUM HAPPINESS AND CONTENTMENT

Cheerful • Contented • Delighted • Excited • Fulfilled • Glad • Gleeful • Gratified • Happy • Healthy self-esteem •

Joyful • Lively • Merry • Optimistic • Playful • Pleased • Proud • Rejuvenated • Satisfied

INTENSE HAPPINESS, CONTENTMENT, AND JOY

Awe-filled • Blissful • Ecstatic • Egocentric • Elated • Enthralled • Euphoric • Exhilarated • Giddy • Jubilant • Manic • Overconfident • Overjoyed • Radiant • Rapturous • Self-aggrandized • Thrilled

REFLECTION QUESTIONS ABOUT YOUR EMOTIONS

As you glance through these emotion families, ask yourself some questions to familiarize yourself with them. If you're keeping an anxiety journal, write down your answers there:

1. Which emotions are easiest for you to work with right now? Which gifts and skills do these easy emotions bring you, and how do you respond when they arise?

2. Which emotions are most challenging for you to work with right now? Which gifts and skills do these challenging emotions bring you, and how do you respond when they arise?

3. How well do you and your anxiety work together? Can you reliably complete your tasks and projects on a deadline, or do you and your anxiety trip over each other right now?

As you enter into an empathic relationship with your emotions, these tables and vocabulary lists will help you unvalence your emotions and welcome their unique genius. When single or multiple emotions arise, come back here to see which gifts and skills your emotions are bringing to you, and identify the intensity level of each emotion you feel with the vocabulary lists. Try asking the internal questions in these tables and see what happens when you engage with your emotions empathically and treat them as natural and necessary parts of your intelligence and your awareness. If you're using a journal, it may help to keep track of what your emotions are doing or saying to you.

Note: Remember that your experience of emotions is unique because you're unique. Your neurology, your upbringing, and your training about emotions all have a significant effect on how you feel and work with them. In this DEI work, I reframe emotions, categorize them to make them more accessible, and teach specific questions and practices to help you work with your emotions in new ways. However, if your emotions don't respond to these practices, you're not doing anything wrong. Your unique emotions are just working in different ways; that's all. If so, I include suggestions for further support in each chapter if you need it.

BUILDING A HEALTHY ENVIRONMENT FOR YOUR EMOTIONS

There are many things you can do to support your emotional health and well-being, and in the next chapter, you'll learn six specific mindfulness practices that will help you work with your emotions empathically and brilliantly. However, self-care and mindfulness are not the only things you need to build yourself a healthy emotional life.

The following questions can help you take a quick inventory of your life when you feel heightened anxiety, or if any of your emotions are intensified or suppressed. If you're working with a journal, you may want to create a page for these questions and track your answers over time. As you track your anxiety and its fellow emotions, these questions may help you pinpoint what your emotions are responding to and what you can do to support them and yourself.

Self-care and mindfulness are marvelous, and at the same time, you and your emotions are affected powerfully by your environment, your relationships, your health, and your whole life. Your emotional health and well-being require a whole-life approach.

How is your sleep?

Sleep is crucial for your emotional well-being, and some research suggests that healthy REM sleep may prune intense emotions from your memories.[5] If you awaken feeling refreshed and ready to start your day, this may mean that you've had a healthy and restorative sleep session. But if you awaken in emotional turmoil, it is possible that you're dealing with an interrupted sleep environment or a sleep difficulty such as insomnia, sleep apnea, or a sleep disorder (depression is also a possibility here). See "Recommended Resources" at the end of this book for good books on sleep.

Are you eating well?

Your emotions respond to changes in your environment, and your environment includes your body. If your eating is unstable and your blood sugar swings throughout the day, your emotions will likely swing as well. For instance, your anxiety may arise if you skip meals because it's worried about your ability to think clearly and perform well. Anxiety may also arise if you overeat (or eat empty calories) because poor eating is taxing to your body and your energy levels, and that's not good for getting things done either. Stabilizing your eating is a great way to stabilize and support your emotions.

What are your movement practices?

We are built for movement, but desk work, driving, and media consumption often require us to be immobile for hours at a time. Resting is important for your health and well-being, but these work- or entertainment-related immobile periods are not usually restful. Movement is good for your bones, your muscles, your balance, your metabolism, and your senses, but it's also good for your emotional health. Movement allows you to express yourself, orient yourself in time and space, and regulate your entire organism. And if you can get out in nature, the benefits of movement are multiplied.

How is your health?

Your overall health, especially your hormonal balance, is intimately involved in your emotional health. As you track your anxiety and its fellow emotions, pay attention to your overall health. Are your emotions being affected by pain, illness, injuries, medications, recreational drugs, alcohol, or caffeine? If your emotions feel troubling or overactive, could they be responding to health conditions or substances that destabilize you or reduce your ability to manage?

Are your intimate relationships healthy?

Your love relationships, friendships, family, and children are a part of your basic emotion-regulation structure. If you've developed healthy relationships with people who respect you, listen to you, and love you, your emotions will have an excellent foundation of support and ease. If you haven't, your emotions may need to protect you at all hours of the day and night.

How is work?

If you work full-time, you spend more time at work than you do in any other place except possibly your bed. You essentially live at work, and it has a tremendous effect on your ability to listen to and work with your emotions. A healthy workplace can contribute to your emotional health, but an unhealthy one can keep your emotions on guard for most of the day (or night). Also, unstable work or unemployment, because they may feel or actually are endangering to your basic survival, will likely require heightened emotional responses as you struggle to care for yourself and meet your responsibilities.

How is your community?

Are you in a healthy community where you feel comfortable and welcome? Your interpersonal relationships are a vital part of your emotional health, and your larger community is as well. A troubled and troubling community may keep your emotions on guard, while a welcoming, functional, and loving community may have a protective effect on your emotions and your overall sense of well-being.

Are you facing uncertainty?

Uncertainty in any area of your life can bring your anxiety forward, and it *should* because there are tasks to complete, preparations to make, ideas to consider, and problems to avoid. If uncertainty exists in many areas of your life, or if it lasts a long time, you and your emotions are going to need to build a myriad of self-care and mindfulness practices (and human support) to help you manage and thrive.

Are you facing inequality, injustice, or abuse?

Inequality, injustice, and abuse will bring several powerful emotions forward to watch over you, protect you, and even save your life. Anxiety and its close friend panic (see chapter 6) will likely need to be on task most of the time, so it's important to increase your self-care practices, seek support, and find a community that understands what you're experiencing and can welcome you, support you, and help you regulate your emotions in the midst of the difficulties you're facing.

Is there anything else?

These questions are a good start, but sometimes you and your emotions will be affected by unique situations. When I awaken feeling troubled or off, I'll stay in bed and ask myself, *What's disturbing me? What's unfinished? What's wrong?* And then I'll wait for the answer to arise before I arise and start my day. In many cases, it's my anxiety reminding me about something that's unfinished or looming, so I begin my day by attending to whatever the problem is. Even if it's just making a list or looking something up online, I do something to attend to whatever my emotions are trying to tell me.

If I could summarize this list in a few words, I'd say this: Pay loving attention to your emotional responses; they'll tell you the truth about what's going on inside you and in your world.

RELYING ON YOUR EMOTIONS TO INCREASE YOUR MINDFULNESS AND SELF-CARE

Your emotions work in every moment to help you make sense of your world and to contribute the skills and intelligence you need in each situation — which is why it's important to build (or find) a healthy and supportive environment for them, yourself, and your loved ones. Your emotions are involved in your relationships and all parts of your social life, and in what I call their *gift-level activation* (which is their softest and most subtle state), your emotions are also involved with your basic self-awareness, mindfulness, self-soothing, and self-care abilities.

In the next chapter, I'll teach you several of my Empathic Mindfulness practices that intentionally engage the gifts and skills in your emotions to help you become grounded, focused, emotionally flexible, self-aware, and socially intelligent. As you learn to work with your anxiety (which can be highly activating, as you may know), these emotion-based practices will help you work with all of your emotions intentionally so that you can access the unique strengths and healing influences they bring to you.

3

Mindfulness Practices for Nurturing Your Emotional Genius

Your anxiety helps you complete your tasks and meet your deadlines, and as it does, it may need to get your attention, point out areas of weakness, fill you with the energy you need to get things done immediately, or challenge your delaying tactics. These are all necessary activities (thank you, anxiety), and though they may feel annoying, disheartening, or overwhelming, they *should* feel that way at times. Getting things done and meeting your responsibilities is often difficult, and it may require a shake-up in your routine, your attitude, or your life; it's hard work.

Anxiety arises to help you with your hard work, but because it can fill you with a great deal of energy and bring other emotions along with it (such as shame or panic), anxiety can sometimes feel like a burden instead of a friend; it can destabilize you. Because of this, it's important to cultivate numerous self-care and mindfulness practices that can help you work with your anxiety (and your other emotions) intentionally and manage your reactions skillfully.

I developed these six Empathic Mindfulness practices over several decades of working directly with my emotions and helping my readers and students do the same.[1] Each of these practices recruits the gifts and skills of one or more of your emotions at their softest level of intensity. I rely on emotions in my mindfulness practices for many reasons, but the most important reasons are that emotions are always freely available, and they work quickly and effectively. These practices can help you stabilize yourself, reframe difficult situations, focus yourself clearly, shift old or unworkable behaviors, and work directly and empathically with your emotions — whenever you need them and wherever you are.

As a highly empathic and sensitive person, I need efficient mindfulness and self-care practices that I can use immediately, on the fly, wherever I am. I don't have time to drop everything and go meditate in a special room or find a quiet, private place; I'm sensitive and empathic all day, every day, and I need quick and simple practices that work. These portable, effective, and supportive practices help people (me included) work directly with emotions and access their gifts and skills at a moment's notice. I can take my time with these practices, but I can also do most of them while I'm driving, during a meeting, at an airport, on stage while I'm teaching, while I'm exercising, and in the middle of a disagreement or a conflict. (Can you tell I'm a task-oriented person?)

As you learn to work with your anxiety and its many fellow emotions, these simple mindfulness practices will help you ground and focus yourself, observe and modify your responses and behaviors, soothe and regulate yourself, and access the genius inside your emotions whenever you need them — and wherever you are. And once you learn them, you can incorporate them into a daily practice or use them as the need arises, whichever works best for you.

You'll find that some of these practices are very easy for you and that you don't really need to do them. That's great; it means that the skills and abilities contained in those practices are already second nature for you. You may also find that some of these practices are difficult or even impossible for you right now. That's important information; it can mean that you need to do some work with the emotions and abilities those practices contain. If you're using a journal, you may want to keep track of your progress and difficulties with each of these practices so that you can witness your changes over time. If you have difficulties, it's okay; this is a learning process.[2]

You may also find that you have your own practices that help you achieve the same states or skills that these practices do. If so, by all means use them; your anxiety will be happy that you've already completed a task (and you can cross it off your list)!

PRACTICE 1: GROUNDING AND FOCUSING

Accessing Your Relaxed and Stable Attention

Being grounded means feeling stable, calm, relaxed, focused, embodied, and integrated. When we talk about *being here now*, it's important to realize that your body is always here now. Your body can remember the past and imagine the future, but it lives only in the present moment. Grounding and Focusing is a simple yet profound body-based practice that can help you be here now instantly, no matter what else is happening around you or within you. You can use this practice when you're feeling anxiety or any other activating emotion — not to repress or erase it, but to help yourself stay present and respond in effective ways when there's a lot going on. This is an especially important practice to use in times of pressure, conflict, or busyness, because it will give you the grounded space you need to gather your resources and act with empathy, focus, and clarity.

This Grounding and Focusing practice uses the soothing and relaxing influence of soft sadness and the instinctive awareness of soft fear to help you feel stable, flexible, and aware. This practice will help you respond intentionally to emotions and situations rather than react haphazardly.

To ground yourself, sit or stand comfortably and breathe in slowly. Don't breathe too deeply (if you're feeling a lot of anxiety, deep breathing may make things worse or cause you to hyperventilate). Just breathe slowly and mindfully. It may help to count to three as you inhale through your nose, and count to five as you slowly exhale through your mouth.

As you inhale, imagine that you're gathering warmth and light inside your body, and as you exhale, imagine that light or warmth moving down through your abdomen and into your hips, thighs, calves, and feet — and then down into the earth. Feel your feet on the floor, and if you're sitting, feel your thighs and your bottom on the chair as well. Continue to breathe and imagine that you're feeling a bit heavier and more anchored.

As you exhale, relax into your body and lean forward a bit. Focus your attention on what it feels like to relax and let go. Scan your body from your head and shoulders down to your arms, your abdomen, your pelvis, your legs, and your feet. If you feel any areas of tension or discomfort, breathe into those areas and let the discomfort fall away into the ground. Keep breathing softly, counting to three on the inhale through your nose and counting to five on the exhale through your mouth, until you feel rooted and aware.

Thank the emotions that help you ground and focus yourself. Thank your soft sadness, which helps you relax, let go, and rejuvenate yourself. And thank your soft fear, which helps meet the present moment with calm and focused awareness.

Stay focused and, if it feels right, make loose spiraling movements with your arms and legs or your entire body as you connect to the ground, and let any tension or discomfort fall away. Grounding and Focusing gives you a simple and efficient way to center yourself, focus yourself, and release excess energy or tension whenever you need to. This is a vital practice to use when your anxiety is activated and on task. Grounding and Focusing can help you work with your activation, soothe yourself regularly, and keep yourself moving forward in a flowing and focused way.

VARIATION: HANDS-ON GROUNDING PRACTICE

When you have a private moment to yourself (or if you need a more physical experience of becoming grounded), you can ground and soothe your body with a type of simple self-massage.

To ground yourself, place your hands on top of your head, and gently run your hands over the sides of your head, down your neck, and down the front of your chest and abdomen. Gently bend forward as you continue running your hands down the front of your thighs and shins. When you reach your feet, imagine brushing downward into the earth.

Stand up and place your hands on top of your head again, and gently run your hands over the sides of your head, down your neck, and down the sides of your trunk to the back of your hips.

As you bend over, run your hands down the back of your bottom, your thighs, your calves, and your ankles. When you reach your heels, imagine brushing downward into the earth. Repeat this process as many times as you like, especially when you've got too many tasks or a deadline is looming; it's like a reset button for your brain and your body, and it can help you return to your tasks with fresh eyes and a clear head.

REFLECTION QUESTIONS ABOUT GROUNDING AND FOCUSING

1. When you feel unfocused and ungrounded, how do you normally respond?

2. What activities, places, people, or animals are naturally grounding for you?

PRACTICE 2: DEFINING YOUR BOUNDARY

Creating Your Healthy Personal Space

Having a defined sense of your boundaries means that you know what's important to you and where you begin and end. Being well-defined in relation to your anxiety can mean that you know how you work best, how to say no to tasks that are not important right now, and how to manage your deadlines in ways that work for you. Your sense of definition can also help you understand which tasks are rightfully yours, and which ones belong to other people. This boundary-defining practice relies on soft anger (which helps you set boundaries around what you value) and soft guilt/shame (which helps you live up to your agreements and treat yourself and others with respect). This practice helps you connect with your body and the present moment because it helps you create a defined sense of where you are in the physical world.

To define your boundaries, sit or stand comfortably and reach your arms straight out to either side of you. (If you cannot use your arms in this way, please use your imagination.)

Imagine that your fingertips are touching the edges of a lighted, oval-shaped bubble that encompasses your private, personal space. Reach your arms out in front of you and then raise them above your head. Your boundary should be an arm's length away from you at all points — in front of you, behind you, on either side of you, above you, and even underneath you. When you can imagine this oval-shaped area all around you, drop your arms and let them relax.

Imagine yourself surrounded by a brightly colored bubble that encompasses your private, personal space at that arm's-length distance — as if you're a yolk standing inside the protective eggshell of your own imagined boundary. Notice whether you normally feel this sense of private space around yourself. Does this arm's-length boundary feel comfortable, or is it too small or too large? You can play with its size to find the most comfortable dimensions.

Get acquainted with your personal boundary; learn where you begin and end — and inhabit this private and defined space where you can work with your own thoughts, sensations, ideas, and emotions. If you can imagine other people inside their own protective boundaries, you'll reinforce your own ability to create proper separations from others. Though this may feel like an imaginary exercise, your brain and your nervous system already map your sense of personal space in every moment. This exercise helps you become aware of and rely on a process that's already occurring.[3]

Your boundary is maintained by your soft anger and your soft guilt/shame. Your soft anger helps you observe and respond to boundary violations that come from outside of you, while soft guilt/shame helps you observe and avoid boundary violations (toward yourself or others) that may come from within you. Setting proper boundaries gives you and everyone around you the space we all need to be our best selves, and it springs from this felt sense of having a private space of your own.

When you're dealing with many tasks or deadlines, or when your anxiety feels intense, ground and focus yourself and check in on your boundaries. What happens to your sense of personal space when you're under pressure or feeling quite anxious? If your boundaries change or disappear, re-establish them and see how your anxiety responds.

REFLECTION QUESTIONS ABOUT YOUR BOUNDARIES

1. Some people set boundaries physically, with their clothing, stance, size, attitude, or tone of voice. Do you have any physical boundary-setting habits?

2. If you know someone with good interpersonal boundaries, how would you describe them?

PRACTICE 3: BURNING CONTRACTS

Channeling All of Your Emotions and Restoring Your Authentic Nature

The Burning Contracts practice helps you channel your emotions and bring outdated, unworkable, or unconscious behaviors and agreements into your conscious awareness where you can change them or release them. This is an especially important practice to use as you work with your anxiety because anxiety helps you live up to your agreements (guilt/shame does, too; see chapter 8). If your agreements aren't workable, or if they're based on out-dated information, your anxiety's adherence to them may waste your time or cause you discomfort or pain. This practice gives you a way to freshen up or clear away those outdated agreements.

To burn a contract, unroll an imaginary piece of blank parchment paper right in front of you (inside your personal boundary). Some people like to imagine that this parchment is rolled out flat on a table, but others like to imagine it in front of them, as if it were a whiteboard or a movie screen. Others want this parchment to have a three-dimensional feel to it, as if it's a basket that can hold anything they place into it. Use whatever idea works best for you. This parchment should have a calming feeling to it or a gentle color that can absorb whatever you place or project onto it. (If this imaginal process doesn't work for you, you can also write your contract on an actual piece of paper as a list, if that feels right.)

Now, you can project, envision, write, speak, or just *think* your agreements onto this parchment — whether they're emotional expectations, intellectual ideas, physical rules, spiritual concepts, or entire relationships. These agreements may be related to your self-image as a person who completes all tasks ahead of time for everyone, no matter how tired you are. Or they may be related to a deadline you agreed to but can't possibly meet. Use whatever emotions arise to move these agreements and behaviors out of unconsciousness and into your conscious awareness.

You can project emotional expectations — how you're supposed to feel and express yourself — onto the parchment. You can project intellectual ideas about how you're supposed to think, what you're supposed to think, or how you're supposed to be intelligent. You can project physical rules about how your body is supposed to look and perform for others. You can project spiritual concepts about how you're supposed to feel, act, and behave in relation to spirituality or religion. Or you can project entire relationships — images of yourself, your partner, and the ways you relate to one another — right onto the parchment. When you can get these behaviors, relationships, and agreements out in front of you, you can begin to observe and individuate from them. In this protected space, you can see yourself not as an unwitting victim of your behaviors or the situations in your life, but as an upright individual who *decides* to act, relate, react, or behave in certain ways and who can now decide to behave differently.

When your parchment (or paper) is full of words, images, feelings, or thoughts, please roll it up tightly so the material inside can't be seen. Toss this rolled-up contract away from you (outside of your personal space) and burn it with whatever emotional energy you feel. You can also tear it into pieces or dispose of it in some other way. This disposal process can help you create a physical sense of separation from outdated and unworkable ideas, and what I've found over the decades is that your emotions will notice this shift and understand that new ideas and new responses are now possible.

I've also found that this seemingly simple process can help people shift their behaviors in a short period of time — weeks or months — even after they've tried and failed for years to shift the behavior through talking. What I've come to understand is that this image-based process accesses emotions where they live — in the area of imagination, symbolic imagery, metaphors, and thoughts that can't really be put into words. You certainly can access your emotions with words (see the next practice), but I've found that deep work with emotions nearly always requires imaginal processes and healing rituals that respect the way emotions work.

Welcome your emotions — whatever they are — and use them to move any outdated or unworkable agreements and behaviors out of the shadows of habit and into your conscious control. Your emotions will provide the precise energy you need to become aware of your contracts, obliterate them, and set yourself free. Repeat this process until you feel a sense of release and completion, and you're done!

After you've burned your contracts, it's a good idea to refill yourself intentionally. The fifth practice in this chapter, Rejuvenation, will help you refresh yourself and reset your intentions to support your new awareness.

REFLECTION QUESTIONS ABOUT BURNING CONTRACTS

1. What kinds of unhealthy contracts do you find yourself agreeing to?

2. What are some healthy contracts you have in your life right now?

3. What is the difference between the situations that lead you to agree to healthy contracts and the situations that lead you to agree to unhealthy ones?

PRACTICE 4: CONSCIOUS COMPLAINING

Giving Voice to the Intelligence in Your Emotions

Conscious Complaining is an emotional channeling practice that gives a voice to your struggles, which can restore your flow, your energy, and your hope. This solo practice helps you access the truth of what you're feeling in a safe and private way, so you can listen to the genius inside your emotions. This practice can also give you a healing break when your anxiety is pushing you, when your guilt and shame are doubting you, when the world feels like too much, or when you're in a mood you can't completely understand.

Most of us are told never to complain because it's allegedly negative; we're supposed to be upbeat and positive instead. I can understand why people are uncomfortable with complaining; however, expecting others to be only positive is emotional repression plus valencing. I created this solitary practice as I was learning to listen to my emotions because I needed to explore my emotions and their messages without other people trying to control me or force me to display only pleasant feelings. I needed my full emotional and intellectual freedom.

What I discovered astonished me: complaining consciously did not make me more cranky, anxious, or depressed. In fact, this practice helped me explore my feelings in complete privacy, hear their messages, and receive their healing gifts. Many researchers have also found that honest expression of emotions carries far greater benefits than enforced positive thinking, which can have a serious backlash effect when it attempts to replace real emotional responses with manufactured pleasant thoughts or affirmations.[4] The positive thinking fad has some valuable aspects to it because we can get ourselves into unhealthy habits of thinking and feeling that require reappraisal. But at its core, positive thinking is a deeply valenced approach to emotions that lifts the Happiness Family above all the other emotions. That's not a positive thing to do.

Notice that I use the word *conscious* before the word *complaining*. This practice brings consciousness and a kind of sacredness to your difficulties, and it helps you do something you likely already do — complain — but now with a clear focus and a deeper, emotionally supportive purpose.

To complain consciously, find a private, solitary place where you can really whine and gripe (or cry) about the frustration, hopelessness, or absurdity of your situation. Start your complaining with a phrase such as "I'm complaining now!" If you're inside, you can complain to the walls or furniture, to a mirror, or to whatever strikes your fancy. If you're outside, you can complain to plants and trees, animals, nature, the sky, the ground, or your God. If you're a frequent complainer, you might want to create a complaining shrine for yourself (maybe on top of a dresser or on an out-of-the-way table), with supportive pictures of grumpy cats, bratty kids, barking dogs, sarcastic cartoons, and whatever else calls to your complaining nature.

I find that it's helpful to complain out loud because my emotions like it when I let my words fly free, but some people enjoy writing down their complaints. Whichever way this practice works for you is the right way. You can also use the Emotional Vocabulary Lists in chapter 2 to find words for the specific intensity levels of each emotion you feel. Remember that a stronger emotional vocabulary — all by itself — can increase your ability to regulate your emotions.

You can complain for as long as you like (you'll be surprised at how quickly this works), then thank whatever you've been whining or grousing at, and end your Conscious Complaining session by bowing, shaking off, and doing something soothing or fun. That's it!

Conscious Complaining gives a voice to your struggles, which restores your flow, your energy, and your hope. When you have full permission to complain within this conscious ceremonial framework, you'll find that your complaints will lead you quickly to the crux of your problems — because you're inviting your emotions to speak freely and share their wisdom with you. With your new level of emotional awareness, you may find that it's much easier to understand and address your struggles and problems. As you incorporate this practice into your life, your anxiety and all of your other emotions will develop their unique voices because there will be a place for them to be heard without repression or criticism. It's much easier to befriend your emotions when they have a voice and you know how to let them express themselves in a safe, private, and well-boundaried practice.

The well-boundaried aspect of this practice is an important part of its healing effect. Conscious Complaining has a clear beginning, middle, and end, which calls you and your emotions to attention. You create a private and safe space so that you're free to feel and say anything you need to (this can be very helpful when you're in a repressive emotional environment). Your emotions — however they show up — are welcome in this practice, which helps you learn about them, listen to them, and befriend them. And speaking the truth in a safe place helps you connect to yourself in a truly healing way.

If you've heard that complaining is terrible and that you should never do it, it's important to know that this may be true for *unconscious* complaining. If you're complaining all day or engaging in endlessly harsh self-talk, you're going to destabilize yourself. It's too much. There's no beginning or end, there are no boundaries, and there's no focused emotional purpose to constant unconscious complaining. But when you set clear boundaries around your complaining practice and build a safe space for it, your emotions can have their say and then go on their merry way because they know you're paying attention to them. In unconscious complaining, you don't really honor or attend to your emotions; instead, you and your emotions just get stuck in an unproductive feedback loop that drags at you. And if you frequently complain (unconsciously) to others, you are likely overburdening them. Bringing consciousness and boundaries to complaining helps you access the gifts of your emotions when you're struggling.

This may sound contradictory, but you just can't be happy or productive — and you can't access the gifts in all of your emotions — unless you complain (consciously) when you truly need to.[5]

REFLECTION QUESTIONS ABOUT CONSCIOUS COMPLAINING

1. What is your current attitude about complaining, and where did you learn it?

2. If you're not allowed to complain, can you burn your contracts with that old agreement? (See "Practice 3: Burning Contracts," on page 62.)

PRACTICE 5: REJUVENATION

Embodying Sacred Space

Rejuvenation is a gentle healing practice that recruits emotions that can soothe and restore you. It's a private and flexible practice that you can perform wherever you are. You can rejuvenate yourself in a few minutes, or you can take as long as you like. Rejuvenation is a wonderful practice to add in your task-focused or deadline-focused anxiety style because it helps you calm, rejuvenate, and reboot yourself so that you can return to your work with a relaxed body and a clear mind. This is also an excellent practice to use after your Burning Contracts practice because it helps you refill and reinhabit the spaces inside you that were once dedicated to outworn or unworkable agreements.

To rejuvenate yourself, imagine your personal boundary as strong, whole, and vibrant. In your personal space, between your skin and the edge of your boundary, imagine your favorite place in nature at your favorite time of day. For instance, feel yourself on a mountainside on a late spring afternoon, beside a creek in a redwood grove at dawn, or on a tropical beach at sunset. Surround yourself with this feeling of beauty, relaxation, and delicious, sensual pleasure. Let your focus drift naturally and embody the way you feel when you're in your favorite place.

As you sense your wonderful nature scene around you, breathe some of these delicious, peaceful feelings into your body. Inhale and imagine breathing the felt sense of this serene and beautiful place into your head and neck. Breathe this feeling down into your chest, your arms, and your hands. Breathe it in through your chest and abdomen and into your lower belly, and breathe it out and down into your legs and feet. Breathe this delightful feeling into every part of your body and fill yourself with this feeling of utter relaxation and beauty.

When you feel full, let your body, your emotions, and your focus soften and relax. You can stay here for as long as you like, but to complete this rejuvenation practice, bend over and touch the floor with both of your hands and let your head hang down. Let go and relax. If you're in public and you can't touch the floor, just take a breath and ground yourself. You're done!

Thank the main emotion that helped you rejuvenate yourself: this is the gift of healthy, flowing joy. Joy arises to help you feel a blissful sense of expansiveness and connection to beauty, pleasure, peace, and wonder. This practice also recruits the gifts of happiness and contentment to fill you with delicious sensations, and it recruits the gifts of jealousy and envy as you identify the most wonderful places, the most wonderful surroundings, and the most wonderful sensations in the world. What's more, rejuvenation also recruits your healthy sadness as you relax, let go, and allow the things you don't need to fall away.

You can surround yourself with this joyful nature scene whenever you like, and you can change up the scene to suit your mood and your needs. Rejuvenation is an all-around emotional healing practice that will help you work with any and all of your emotions. It's especially useful during periods of anxiety-driven hard work because this rejuvenation practice helps you take a break with your emotions rather than running away from them and losing your connection to their genius.

REFLECTION QUESTIONS ABOUT REJUVENATION

1. What are your current beliefs about self-care (and do those beliefs need an update with Burning Contracts)?

2. How many rejuvenating self-care activities do you perform on a daily basis?

3. What gets in the way of your rejuvenating activities, if anything?

PRACTICE 6: RESOURCING

Developing Bodily Sources of Comfort and Empowerment

There is a wonderful and simple practice that I derived from the Somatic Experiencing® therapy created by trauma-healing expert

Dr. Peter Levine.[6] This practice can help you find healing resources inside yourself, especially during painful or troubling times. You can perform this practice anywhere, and you can complete it in less than a minute, or you can extend it into a luxurious practice and take as long as you like. Resourcing is especially helpful when you need to feel your anxiety (because it's helping you get things done) and also to feel other emotions or other sensations at the same time. This practice can help you be here now in a new way.

How to resource yourself: At any time of the day or night, no matter where you are or what's going on, there are places in your body that feel strong, stable, capable, and resourceful. Even when you're in pain or when you're dealing with extreme difficulties, there are strong and calm areas in your body that you can access intentionally. Let's try this now.

Sit quietly, with your eyes open or closed, and feel into the words *strong*, *stable*, and *resourceful*. Locate an area in your body that feels this way right now. This can be a large area like your abdomen or your thighs, or a small area like your left foot or the upper part of your right arm. Where does this feeling reside in your body in this moment? Right now, where do you feel strong, stable, and resourceful?

Focus on this area and breathe as you feel into this innate and effortless sense of strength and stability that already exists inside you. These qualities belong to you. They're available to you at any time, and in any situation.

Now, focus on an area of tightness or discomfort and get a sense of its qualities. Is it sharp, dull, hot, cold, constricted, or loose? Observe it gently and describe how it feels. Breathe into it softly and then move back and forth between your area of discomfort and your area of stability and resourcefulness — not to erase one or the other, but to open your focus to include both areas. This is Resourcing. It's simple, and yet it's nearly revolutionary because very few of us ever learned how to connect to the preexisting strength, calm, and resourcefulness that exist inside our own bodies.

Resourcing is nearly opposite to the way most of us have learned to behave around pain and trouble. Usually, pain and trouble will pull all of our attention, and we'll focus everything on it. There's a way that pain and trouble can dampen or silence the parts of you that feel fine, strong, and resourceful. And in the presence of pain and trouble, it's easy to hyperfocus on difficulties and lose your awareness of the fact that you also have sources of comfort inside you that are fully accessible, right now.

With Resourcing, you can learn how to pay attention to more than one thing. So, if you have a horrible headache, you can use Resourcing — not to pretend that your headache is gone, but to open your focus to include the comfort that exists in (for instance) your arm or your knee. Or if you're feeling cranky and impatient, yet there's nothing you can do but wait, you can focus on a place inside yourself that has all the time in the world and feels fine. Resourcing can help you remember that you have choices, and that you contain many things — and many resources — in the same moment.

VARIATION: RESOURCING WITH YOUR ANXIETY

If you're dealing with intense anxiety, you can focus inside yourself and find an area in your body that feels calm and grounded right now — not to repress your anxiety, but to open your focus to include the physical sense of unhurried stability that exists inside you during anxious times. This may help your anxiety take a moment and focus its genius on what's important. This is a simple practice, but as you and your anxiety become friends and partners, your anxiety will learn to take your lead when you need to calm and soothe yourself. With Resourcing, you can care for yourself without repressing your anxiety or treating it as a problem. Resourcing opens your options and your awareness, and it treats your emotions with love and respect.

Resourcing doesn't repress the fact of what you're experiencing. Instead, Resourcing helps you connect to other facts, which are that more than one thing is going on and that you always have the resources you need to deal with whatever confronts you.

Resourcing is naturally grounding and focusing, and it helps you set internal boundaries around emotional and social stimuli. With Resourcing, you can feel a powerful emotion and also sense the calming strength of (for instance) your calves. Or when you're in the presence of someone who's in emotional turmoil, you can experience their difficulty and also connect to your own inner sources of grounding, peace, and stability. Resourcing gives you ways to clearly identify difficulties *and* clearly identify your extensive internal resources in the exact same moment.

Resourcing is a wonderful self-soothing behavior that can and does coexist with difficulties, and it can help you learn that one condition or emotional state doesn't erase another. Resourcing can help you open your focus to include trouble and difficulties in the full-bodied narrative of your whole life, rather than hyperfocus on the troubles and lose your perspective and your skills (or run from your troubles and hyperfocus on the happy-peppy side of life).

Resourcing is also a supportive practice to use when you're unable to sleep. Instead of struggling to clear your mind or fretting about how you *really* need to get some sleep (hello, anxiety), Resourcing can help you locate areas of your body that are tired and ready to sleep. You can feel your bed beneath you and let yourself sink into your mattress while you allow your anxiety to be concerned about your sleep. Even if you don't immediately fall into sleep, Resourcing is a wonderful way to achieve relaxation during sleepless periods.[7]

Resourcing can help you learn to identify multiple internal states and transition gracefully between them, and this will help you create and maintain a healthy internal environment for yourself. This internal resourcefulness is vital to your ability to work with powerful emotions like anxiety, because it teaches you how to work in partnership with your emotions and make choices when they arise instead of throwing yourself away or losing your composure in response to them. Resourcing can help you create a healing and portable inner sanctuary that's available to you whenever and wherever you need it — no matter what else is going on inside or outside of you.

REFLECTION QUESTIONS ABOUT RESOURCING

1. Do you currently have a grounded and focused (rather than distracted or disconnected) way to soothe yourself during difficulties or upheavals?

2. Do you have any people or situations in your life that are resources for you?

MAKING THESE PRACTICES A PART OF YOUR LIFE

These six practices can help you befriend your emotions and integrate them into your everyday life so that you'll have easy access to their gifts, skills, and genius whenever you need them.

As you learn these practices, you can create a schedule for yourself, or you can use them whenever you need them. If you're using a journal, it may help you to create a page for each practice and track your progress with them over time. Some people swear by a daily routine, but they're likely task-oriented people who are suggesting something that would work for them. If you're more deadline-oriented, you may want to give yourself a date to learn them by or create some other approach that makes sense to your anxiety. Your learning process should work for you.

It's important to use these practices in your everyday life, and especially when you're struggling. When your anxiety arises and you feel unsettled, see if the Grounding and Focusing practice helps. You can do it in a split second once you learn the process. Defining Your Boundary can also help you reset yourself if you become frazzled, and it can also be done in a split second.

You can perform a quick Resourcing practice during tense times and find an area inside you that feels relaxed and unhurried so that you can expand your focus and know that you've got many inner resources. Or you can perform a simple Rejuvenation practice and imagine yourself in a beautiful natural area where you can breathe freely.

Conscious Complaining is great to do in the car if you're alone, and it can also be a silent, interior practice of grousing to yourself if you need to. I often do this when I'm on stage and there are a lot of things going on. On stage, I must appear professional, engaged, and empathic, but inside myself, I have complete freedom to feel and express anything, including annoyance, sadness, fatigue, confusion, or apathy. Silent Conscious Complaining is a great way to reset myself without repressing my emotions.

Burning Contracts is a lengthier process, but I've written out the details of an uncomfortable contract during lectures and meetings, to be destroyed or burned later. These might include being agreeable when I don't feel agreeable; working too late and missing out on relaxation time; snapping at people instead of sharing what's going on with me; forgetting to eat; perfectionism; missing my workouts this week; constantly repressing my sadness; and so forth. If you're working with a journal, you can keep a series of Burning Contracts pages where you can write down unworkable behavioral contracts you'd like to burn.

I'll revisit these practices throughout this book and remind you about ways to support yourself when your anxiety and its fellow emotions gather to help you do your best work.

Note: If these practices don't work for you, you're not failing at empathic mindfulness. You're unique, and you may respond better to different approaches. If you read through these practices and know a different or easier way to achieve these same states or perform similar processes, then by all means use what works best for you.

In the next chapter, you'll learn a specific practice for anxiety that will help you gather and organize all of its information so that you can complete your tasks and meet your deadlines skillfully.

4

The Power of Consciously Questioning Your Anxiety

Your anxiety can see and imagine the future, and it can also see and build a detailed list of all the problems that may occur along the way. All of them. *All. Of. Them.* If you had a friend who could perform this remarkable feat of future projection, you would probably value her for the time and money she saves you. But when this friend is in your head, keeping you up late, waking you up early, or talking in your ear, it can be too much. And yet, this too-muchness isn't the fault of anxiety. As we often do with emotions, many of us will mistakenly blame anxiety as if it *causes* the trouble, when in fact anxiety arises to help us *deal with* the trouble.

Getting your tasks done, meeting your deadlines, and keeping tabs on your responsibilities can be a long slog through rough terrain every now and then. Your anxiety will bring you the energy and focus you need during these difficult times; however, the addition of increased anxiety on top of too many tasks, too many looming deadlines, and too many responsibilities may make anxiety seem like a distressing presence instead of a helpful one. Conscious Questioning is an anxiety-specific practice that helps you bring all of anxiety's information out into the open, where you can organize and respond to it skillfully.

This practice won't turn your anxiety into something it's not. You'll still feel activated because you *should* feel activated. That's the point of anxiety. But your activation doesn't need to be destabilizing or painful. The focus of this practice is not to move you to a state of calmness or get rid of your anxiety; instead, it's an emotional-channeling practice that respects your anxiety and helps you work with it intentionally and successfully.

Note: This simple practice focuses on what I call *situational anxiety*, or anxiety that arises to help you complete your tasks or meet your deadlines. If this Conscious Questioning practice doesn't help, or if you feel more agitated in response to it, there's likely another emotion (or emotions) working alongside your anxiety. In part II, we'll explore nine emotions that work with anxiety (or against it, depending on the situation), and you'll learn new strategies for working with your anxiety when other emotions are present.

FIRST UP: SOME LIST-MAKING SUGGESTIONS

List making is an art, but it's a deeply individual one. Some people create an organized, step-by-step list and cross off each completed item with a feeling of contentment and relief. Others create a circular or seemingly disorganized list that visually represents many different activities and ideas and serves as a loose guideline in which items may never be crossed off. Still others create a list of lists and sublists that spread out over their workspace. There are many ways to organize your tasks and projects, and the important thing to ask yourself about your lists is whether they help you get things done on time. If they don't, it's time to try a different approach.

If your loose and circular style doesn't help you focus, try making lists that are organized by priority or by project. Or if your very organized lists increase your anxiety but don't help you get things done, maybe walk away from list making for a few days to see how you do. Also, pay attention to your anxiety style: if you're task focused, it may help you to write down your tasks in a step-by-step way, and perhaps chronologically or in order of importance. If you're deadline focused, you can write out the many aspects of your projects, and if you need help getting things done, you can create intermediate deadlines in a longer project. When you can understand and support your own anxiety style, you can create lists that make sense to you and your anxiety, even if they don't make sense to anyone else.

My late mother, Kara Hubbard, had a task-focused anxiety style and was a list maker extraordinaire. Nearly every day started with her writing out a list in perfect cursive handwriting; it was a ritual for her. She also found a trick that gave her a sense of completion, which was to write down something simple at the top of the list, such as "wake up" or "make a list." She laughed about it, but crossing off that first item prepared her (and her anxiety) beautifully for the day ahead.

In the 1980s, Mom discovered a list-making concept called *mind mapping* that was popular at the time, and she tried it because there were exciting promises about how it would improve creativity, efficiency, and focus. You may have seen this process, where you write down your main idea or project in the middle of a page and radiate ideas out from there with lines and circles and different colors. My feeling is that mind mapping was created for deadline-focused procrastinators because mind maps confuse me and increase my anxiety! I can't stand them. Mom worked with mind maps for a few months, but soon her mind maps were lined up like her lists. Mind maps are an interesting idea, but they don't work for everyone, and neither would my mom's careful lists. We're all unique.

The important thing is to find a way to write things down so that your anxiety knows that you're on the case and that it doesn't have to hold every last detail in your working memory. If you deal with a lot of circling or cycling anxieties, writing things down (in a way that works for you) can help your anxiety settle and feel less burdened.

It can be especially helpful to prioritize your lists in order of *now*, *later*, and *whenever* so that you don't crowd your lists with things that aren't true priorities. During writing projects, when I sometimes forget to eat, drink, water the plants, or return phone calls, I put up a sign that says *Living things first*. It helps me set healthy priorities when I'm hyperfocused.

When you find a writing process that helps your anxiety organize itself, you'll be able to work more skillfully with everyday anxieties about getting things done. But if your anxiety still needs some support — for instance, if the things you're anxious about are too far in the future, too uncertain, or too complex — the following Conscious Questioning for Anxiety practice can help.

CONSCIOUS QUESTIONING FOR ANXIETY

Anxiety helps you prepare for the future, and it acts as your task-completion emotion and your deadline alert system. As you know, anxiety can be powerfully action focused, so expressing it when it's intense can be pretty tricky; it can run you in five different directions at once. However, repressing anxiety isn't a very good option either, because anxiety has *work* to do; repression might slow it down for a minute, but it will still need to do its work. When any of your emotions are intense, it may feel tempting to either express them all over the place or shut them down and repress them, but you can make significant changes if you can take three simple steps:

1. Name your emotion(s) precisely.

2. Engage empathically with your emotion(s) so that it can do its proper work.

3. Ask for help if your emotion(s) won't shift.

The simple act of naming your emotions can help you focus and stabilize yourself. With anxiety, you might say, "Okay, I'm anxious, and that means something needs my attention." This naming step can help you focus yourself and down-regulate your activation because you can identify what you're feeling as anxiety and not an alarming physical condition.

Then, to engage empathically with your anxiety, you pay attention to how it works and lean into its gifts and skills. This Conscious Questioning practice helps you engage intentionally with anxiety, and it helps you identify each of the issues your anxiety is responding to so that you can organize all of your tasks, concerns, and ideas. This practice will also help you ground and refocus yourself *with* your anxiety (rather than despite it).

You can begin this practice by asking yourself (out loud) about each of the things that truly need to get done. The word *truly* is key because if you merely ask your anxiety what needs to get done, it might answer: "Check the stove to see if you turned it off, now take out the garbage, now wash your hands, now check your mail, and what about reorganizing the closets or starting a carpentry project? Oh, did you check the stove?" And then it's four hours later, and you've been sent on any number of pointless errands. Anxiety, did those things *truly* need to get done?

But if you're repressing or ignoring your anxiety and you ask yourself what needs to get done, something inside you may answer: "Eat chocolate, browse the web, drink some wine, numb out, and watch TV!" And again, it's four hours later, and where are you? Anxiety, what *truly* needs to get done?

It's also helpful to write things down. Beyond your more focused list making, writing in a stream-of-consciousness way can help you mindfully express your anxieties, become aware of them, and organize them physically. This may seem like a simplistic activity, but it's specifically suited to what anxiety does, why it arises, and how it works; writing down (or voicing) your anxieties will help your anxiety organize itself. Attending to your anxiety in this way is an emotionally intelligent action that helps your anxiety settle down a bit, so you can ground and focus yourself on what needs to get done. With this quick and focused practice, you can access the gifts in your anxiety, identify any upcoming tasks or projects, and organize everything you need to do to complete them.

How to Consciously Question Your Anxiety

Begin your Conscious Questioning session with a clear statement, such as, "Okay, I'm consciously questioning my anxiety now." Remember to write down your answers so that you can channel your anxiety intentionally. If you need some support, here are some helpful questions you might ask about the things your anxiety is focusing on:

- What are my strengths and resources?
- Do I need more information?
- Are there any upcoming deadlines?
- What do I need to do to prepare?
- Is anything unfinished?
- Have I achieved or completed something similar in the past?
- Can I contact (or read about) someone who has successfully done this thing?
- Is there anything I've overlooked?
- Can I delegate any tasks or ask for help?
- What is one small task I can complete right now?
- When you feel done, end your Conscious Questioning session with a clear statement such as, "Thanks, anxiety! I'm done now."

When you're done, do one or more of the tasks that you and your anxiety have identified, and also do something that's fun, grounding, or soothing. The Hands-On Grounding practice is quick and comforting, and the Rejuvenation practice can also help you spend some healing imaginal time in your favorite place and breathe its soothing atmosphere into your body. It's important to create regular rest and relaxation breaks when your anxiety needs to be on point and on the job, because too much focus is just as destabilizing as too little. With anxiety and every other emotion, balance is the key.

Anxiety is always looking out for you and trying to help you, but it needs your loving guidance and support in order to do its best work. One of our DEI mottos, which my anxiety and I created during an intense time of heavy work and deadlines is this:

There's always enough time for every important thing.

When I get spun out by too much work, I write this motto down and place it where I (and my anxiety) can see it. This idea — that I have enough time, combined with the word *important* — helps me and my emotions reset and refocus on what's truly vital and meaningful. In anxious times, I've found that focusing on what's important and meaningful helps reduce my sense of too-muchness and points me in the direction I've been meaning to go.

IF THIS PRACTICE INCREASES, CONFUSES, OR DEADENS YOUR ANXIETY

Conscious Questioning is a simple practice because situational anxiety is a simple emotion. Anxiety's job is clear and well-defined: it helps you look ahead, marshal your resources, complete your tasks, and meet your deadlines. Conscious Questioning supports the work your anxiety is already doing so that you can channel it in appropriate and anxiety-specific directions.

However, anxiety doesn't just work in the exterior world of jobs and calendars; it also works in your interior world of emotions, inner struggles, and past difficulties or traumas. This is an excellent and supportive thing for anxiety to do, but it's not something that most of us have heard about or learned to identify. There are a lot of reasons for our ignorance about anxiety's everyday connection to other emotions and past struggles. Valencing emotions as positive or negative is certainly a main culprit in our enforced emotional ignorance, and so is our tendency to use expression and repression to throw our emotions away. But to my eye, a huge stumbling block is our very poor emotional vocabulary, which obscures the normal behavior of mixed emotions. Remember that there are only four words in the English language that describe multiple emotions: *bittersweet, gloating, nostalgic,* and *ambivalent.* While these are excellent words, they can't possibly help us understand how anxiety works with its fellow emotions.

As we explore many different emotions that work alongside anxiety (either to support its task-and-deadline focus, or to alert you to something that needs your attention), I'll create new blended emotion words for fun. English needs many blended words for emotions so that we can observe and understand how anxiety and its fellow emotions work together to help us complete our inner and outer tasks.

It's important to know that in many mixed-emotion situations, increased activation is often necessary (even if it's uncomfortable or destabilizing) because something needs your attention. Your Empathic Mindfulness practices such as Grounding and Focusing or Resourcing can help you create an inner environment where you can engage with and support your emotions — and figure out what's going on. You should certainly ask for help if your mixed emotions won't shift, but I find that when you can approach your emotions with love and empathy, most of them will engage with you and each other in ways that you can understand and work with. In many cases, you can ask for help with your emotions from your emotions themselves.

IF YOU FEEL MORE ACTIVATED OR OVERWHELMED AFTER THIS PRACTICE

If you feel any sense of dread or overwhelm after you try this practice, two emotions in your Fear Family may be involved: check in with your fear in chapter 5, or your panic in chapter 6. If dread is present, then panic (which arises to help you deal with trauma) will usually be involved, but it's good to check in with your fear as well (fear helps you identify change, novelty, and possible hazards in your immediate environment). Chapters 5 and 6 contain supportive practices for these mixed emotions.

If you feel pressure or a sense of crabbiness or rage, check in with your anger in chapter 7. Anger helps you identify what's valuable and meaningful, and it helps you set your boundaries clearly. Your anger may be paired up with your anxiety because people and things are in your way or because there's more to do than any one person could possibly handle. Chapter 7 can help you learn to set clear boundaries around your tasks and projects.

You may also feel excited or hyperactivated if any of the emotions in your Happiness Family are involved (happiness, contentment, or joy; see chapter 10). Valencing teaches us to see these three emotions as only positive, but just as it is with every other emotion, they each have an upside and a downside.

Happiness helps you feel delight and amusement and look forward to a bright future, but it can also lead you to agree to too many things in the present because it's all so delightful! Contentment helps you feel proud of yourself for a job well done, but if it's unbalanced, you may think you're more prepared than you truly are, or you may overburden yourself with projects just to feel good about yourself. Joy is a peak state that connects you with bliss and transcendence, and it's a marvelous moment in time, but it's not meant to be an everyday emotion. If your joy is involved with your anxiety, it can lead you into a limitless ecstatic state where you may agree to projects or relationships that have nothing whatsoever to do with your real life. Sometimes that's marvelous, and sometimes that's a disaster, so it's important to keep your wits about you when joy arises. Chapter 10 can help you approach the emotions in your Happiness Family with care, kindness, and emotional skills.

IF YOU FEEL LESS FOCUSED AFTER THIS PRACTICE

If you feel spacey or unable to focus after you use this Conscious Questioning practice, check in with your confusion in chapter 5. Confusion helps you take a break when there's too much to do (or too much input coming at you) or when you're overly focused. You need balance in your task-completion behaviors and full permission to zone out and give yourself breaks from focus. Your confusion often arises to bring balance to high-intensity situations.

You may also feel spacey if two emotions in your Happiness Family are involved (happiness and joy) because both tend to want more, yes, yay! See chapter 10 to learn how to maintain your healthy focus when happiness and joy are active.

IF YOU FEEL DE-ENERGIZED OR LESS PREPARED AFTER THIS PRACTICE

If you lose your energy and your ability to move forward, check on your situational depression in chapter 9. Depression arises when something in your life cannot work, and it will often reduce your energy and your ability to move forward. If you tend to procrastinate and not finish things (remember that procrastination is perfectly fine as long as you meet your deadlines), your depression may be active. Depression and anxiety can seem to be diametrically opposed emotions, but the paradox they create can lead to creativity and renewal if you can treat both emotions (and yourself) with love and empathy.

If you doubt yourself and feel unable to proceed, check in with your shame in chapter 8. Your shame arises when you're not living up to your agreements or your ethics — or when your agreements and ethics need to be updated because they're not workable or livable. If you procrastinate and fail to meet your deadlines, you may want to look at how your shame and your anxiety work together. Shame can be painful, but it's not an intrinsically negative emotion (there are no negative emotions). The reason we mistakenly identify shame as negative is that it arises to help us deal with negative and painful situations. We've learned (wrongly) to blame shame for the pain, but shame doesn't *bring* the trouble; it arises to help you *deal with* the trouble. See chapter 8 for support with your shame.

IF YOU DON'T FEEL LIKE READING RIGHT NOW

If you feel destabilized and don't want to read right now, that's okay. If your emotions don't feel workable, take good care of yourself. You can use the practices in this book to engage with your emotions, ask their specific questions, and develop your Empathic Mindfulness skills, but if your emotions won't settle down, you're not failing! We all need help to regulate our emotions and deal with our difficulties. I know that professional mental health care is a luxury for many people, but fortunately, talking things through with a trusted friend or loved one can soothe your emotions and help you feel more at ease. If you need more information and support, the HelpGuide website (helpguide.org) is a great place to start.

If you're ready to move forward, the next chapter will help you learn how to tell the difference between anxiety and its family members *fear*, *confusion*, and *panic*. Knowing which emotion (or emotions) you're feeling will help you develop stronger emotion regulation skills, certainly, but it will also help you know which forms of emotional genius are being brought to bear on your situation.

PART II

When
ANXIETY
Teams Up with
Other Emotions

5

The Difference Between
Fear, Confusion, Panic,
and Anxiety

Anxiety is a member of the Fear Family, which collectively brings you the gifts of intuition, instincts, orienting, and taking effective action. Sadly, most people don't know much about the Fear Family, and they tend to valence the entire family negatively — which leads them to avoid or suppress these emotions. Accordingly, many people clump all of the emotions in the Fear Family into one shapeless (and highly activated) emotion. This is a mistake because the Fear Family contains vital and unique emotions that need to be untangled so that you can work with them appropriately.

Learning to identify your emotions is an important part of learning how to regulate them, and in regard to anxiety and the Fear Family, knowing which emotion you're feeling can mean the difference between completing your tasks successfully or losing your focus completely. It's crucial to know the difference between fear, anxiety, confusion, and panic if you want to work well with any of them.

Let's look again at four of the emotions from the Fear Family table so that you can see them together and understand how they interrelate. I've moved envy and jealousy out of the table for this chapter because, even though they're vital emotions, I'm not focusing on jealousy or envy in this book. They deserve their very own book!

Emotion	Gifts and Skills	Internal Questions
FEAR arises to help you focus on **the present moment**, access your instincts and intuition, and tune in to changes in your immediate environment.	Intuition, instincts, focus, clarity, attentiveness, readiness	*What action should be taken?*
ANXIETY (*or WORRY*) is focused on **the future**. It arises to help you look ahead and identify the tasks you need to complete and the deadlines you need to meet.	Foresight, focus, task completion, procrastination alert!	*What brought this feeling forward?* *What **truly** needs to get done?*
CONFUSION is a mask for fear and anxiety that arises when you have too much to process all at once. Confusion can give you a much-needed time-out.	Soft awareness, spaciness, flexibility, taking a time-out	*What is my intention?* *What action should be taken?*

Emotion	Gifts and Skills	Internal Questions
PANIC arises when you face threats to your survival. Panic gives you three lifesaving choices: *fight, flee,* or *freeze.*	Sudden energy, intense attention, absolute stillness, survival	During an emergency: *Just listen to your body.* Fight, flee, or freeze. Your body is a survival expert, and it will keep you safe. For panic that relates to past difficulties or traumas: *What has been frozen in time?* *What healing action must be taken?*

Notice that all of the emotions in the Fear Family are connected to taking action in some way. The difference between fear and anxiety relates to time. Fear helps you focus on *the present moment* and your instincts so that you'll know which action to take. Anxiety helps you focus on *the future* and your responsibilities so that you can complete your tasks and meet your deadlines. Panic helps you fight, flee, or freeze to protect your life (or the lives of others) in hazardous situations, and it helps you choose healing actions in response to unresolved traumas from your past. Confusion acts as a mask for fear and anxiety, and it reduces your focus so that you can't take decisive actions when too much input is coming at you — too many tasks, too much data, or too many deadlines. Confusion can give you a much-needed break if you know how to work with it, or it can knock you off track if you don't. I think that's true for all emotions: when you know how to work with them, you can flow with the gifts they bring you instead of being overwhelmed by them.

When you understand how and why your emotions work, you can befriend them and empathize with them.

Engaging empathically with your emotions as your friends and guides does many things for you. It calms you and gives you a sense of partnering with your emotions instead of being their master or their puppet. Identifying your emotions with precision helps you develop better self-awareness and stronger emotion-regulation skills (simply naming your emotions can reset your entire system so that you can focus). And asking respectful questions of your emotions means that you won't tend to throw more emotions (such as shame, depression, or panic) into the mix because you'll be focused on what's happening instead of judging the fact that you have human emotions.

Unvalencing your emotions and learning to channel them means reframing them and learning to respond to them in loving and empathic ways. When you can do this, you can work with whichever emotions arise without adding more activation or reactivity on top of them. Your empathic approach to your emotions is the key to working skillfully with your anxiety, no matter which other emotions are present.

FEAR AND ANXIETY: THE DIFFERENCE BETWEEN BEING HERE NOW AND BEING THERE THEN

Fear and anxiety are siblings, yet each has a specific job to do: fear focuses on the present moment, and anxiety focuses on the future.

Emotion	Gifts and Skills	Internal Questions
FEAR arises to help you focus on **the present moment**, access your instincts and intuition, and tune in to changes in your immediate environment.	Intuition, instincts, focus, clarity, attentiveness, readiness	*What action should be taken?*
ANXIETY (*or WORRY*) is focused on **the future**. It arises to help you look ahead and identify the tasks you need to complete or the deadlines you need to meet.	Foresight, focus, task completion, procrastination alert!	*What brought this feeling forward?* *What **truly** needs to get done?*

The Grounding and Focusing practice relies on the softest levels of activation in your sadness and fear. Grounding and Focusing helps you remain flexible, calm, and grounded as you tune in to your senses and your instincts about the present moment and your immediate environment. This practice can also help you soothe and stabilize yourself so that you can work skillfully with your anxiety and think clearly about the future.

Fear and anxiety regularly work together (*fearxiety?*), because when you have a task to do, that task is both out in the future (where your anxiety keeps an eye on it) and in the present moment (where your fear searches your environment for any changes, new data, or possible obstacles). To successfully complete a task or meet a deadline, you have to be in two places at once: you need to be in the present moment making smart decisions, and you need to be out in the future, planning for something that hasn't happened yet. *Fearxiety* is an energized (and perhaps unsettling) state to be in, and your Empathic Mindfulness practices can help you gather that energy and channel it in a purposeful way. Grounding and Focusing will help.

New students usually ask me how often they should ground themselves, and the answer is most of the time. Being grounded means having access to the calming and releasing gifts of soft sadness, while being focused means having access to the instinctive and intuitive gifts of soft fear. These emotional skills are nearly always appropriate and supportive. There are times when it's fine to be ungrounded and unfocused (we all need time to float and relax), but you definitely want to be able to ground and focus yourself at will. Grounding and Focusing helps you work with emotions, sensations, and situations from a place of calm and clarity. Luckily, your soft sadness and fear are available to you wherever and whenever you need them (thank you, sadness and fear).

Being grounded and focused is especially important when you're dealing with situations that require social insight, such as cultural differences, unequal social relationships, or unsafe situations that you need to navigate skillfully. These situations will activate your *fearxiety* because you need the support of your insight, instincts, and intuition about what is happening, what may happen, and how you can act and react. Grounding and Focusing increases your social insight and helps you observe your social situations clearly so that you can react nimbly.

Your social insight in unequal or uncomfortable situations is often pitched at a higher frequency than it is when you're among familiar people who treat you as an equal. It's hard work to remain vigilant in social situations, and this work, which sociologist Arlie Hochschild calls "emotional labor," may in turn activate and exhaust you.[1] If your social situation is unsafe, your *fearxiety* may also intensify and activate your panic, so the grounding portion of this practice becomes not just a good idea, but a regular self-care tool. If you do a lot of emotional labor in unequal or unsafe social environments, see chapter 12 for ways to support yourself and your emotions in difficult situations and difficult times.

WORKING WITH ANXIETY AND FEAR TOGETHER

When *fearxiety* is present, you'll be aware of and focused on the present moment, and you'll also be aware of and focused on your upcoming responsibilities in the future. Fear and anxiety help you take effective actions. When you feel *fearxiety*, you may feel comfortably focused and on point, you may feel hyped up and ready to go, or you may feel rattled and agitated. In some cases, you may feel confused and unable to focus (see "Confusion and Anxiety" on page 104), or you may ramp up into a feeling of dread or impending danger (see "Panic and Anxiety" on page 110). If you need help identifying where you are on the continuum, see the Emotional Vocabulary Lists in chapter 2 and find the words that most closely match your level of activation in each emotion. It's important, no matter how your *fearxiety* feels, to ground and focus yourself (if you can't ground or focus, see "Panic and Anxiety" on page 110) and to orient to each emotion in turn. Then, you can channel your fear and anxiety simply by asking the internal questions for each of them:

FEAR: *What action should be taken?*

ANXIETY: *What brought this feeling forward? What **truly** needs to get done?*

Notice that both questions are about action, but the anxiety question helps you prioritize your action. When *fearxiety* is present, you may be highly activated, and it's important to channel that activation in an intentional and workable way. In some *fearxiety* situations, you might overbalance toward your fear and the present moment and do task after task without any meaningful goal, and though you *will* get things done, your tasks may not add up to anything useful. You need your anxiety's future-facing input to help you complete the tasks that truly need to get done. The anxiety questions will help you channel your energy in efficient ways so that you can complete your important tasks *and* meet your deadlines.

Or you may overbalance toward anxiety and the future, lose your present-time focus, and do anything *but* your tasks, which may be relaxing but inefficient. Your fear can help you refocus on the present moment, ground yourself in what needs to happen now, and make decisions about present-time actions that will be helpful (for instance, you may simply need to rest).

When you know what has brought your *fearxiety* forward, what actions your fear requires (this can include choosing not to act), and what your anxiety truly needs to get done, then you can make emotionally appropriate decisions and take actions that respect your fear *and* your anxiety. When you've listened to and channeled both emotions, your fear and anxiety may recede to their soft states until you need their more intense gifts once again. This can be a surprisingly quick process once you get the hang of treating your emotions as your friends and guides. When you can name your emotions precisely and treat them with respect, they'll often contribute their gifts quickly and step back until you need them again. Your Grounding and Focusing practice will help you create a calm and resourceful inner environment where this kind of emotional virtuosity can flourish.

List making is an anxiety-specific healing practice, and both your fear and your anxiety may settle down when you make a list of all the things they're alerting you to. Research on anxiety has suggested that writing out your anxieties and making lists about the things you need to do feel like actions to your body.[2] The simple act of writing itself seems to signal to your anxiety that you're on the job; in response to your list-making actions, your anxiety will often return to its soft and watchful state.

If list making or your Grounding and Focusing practice increases your anxiety or creates upheavals within your emotional realm, your anxiety may be partnered up with panic, shame, or depression; we'll explore those emotional relationships in the chapters ahead.

When *fearxiety* is present, you'll have access to your instincts in the present moment and your planning abilities in the future. These are marvelous and necessary skills that you can rely on in every area of your life. There *will be* activation because these are two action-oriented emotions, but your Grounding and Focusing practice — and your ability to work respectfully with both emotions — can help you remain focused and stable in the presence of your *fearxiety*.

CONFUSION AND ANXIETY: KNOWING HOW TO LET YOURSELF REST

People often mistake confusion for anxiety, especially when their heads are swirling with facts, ideas, and concerns that won't line up in any kind of order. Anxiety and confusion can join together (*confusiety?*), but they are very different emotional states with different purposes. You might even say that they bring you contrasting gifts: on one hand, anxiety sharpens and increases your energy and focus, and on the other hand, confusion reduces your focus so that your awareness becomes hazy and uncertain. Because these two emotions are so different, you might feel disoriented when they appear together (or when they oscillate back and forth with one another).

Emotion	Gifts and Skills	Internal Questions
CONFUSION is a mask for fear and anxiety that arises when you have too much to process all at once. Confusion can give you a much-needed time-out.	Soft awareness, spaciness, flexibility, taking a time-out	*What is my intention?* *What action should be taken?*
ANXIETY (*or WORRY*) is focused on **the future**. It arises to help you look ahead and identify the tasks you need to complete or the deadlines you need to meet.	Foresight, focus, task completion, procrastination alert!	*What brought this feeling forward?* *What **truly** needs to get done?*

When *confusiety* appears, you may be dealing with a situation of overwhelm: too many tasks, too many deadlines, or too many ideas. The key to working with both emotions is to rely on each of them for what it does best. You can learn to welcome the restful and down-regulating aspects of confusion so that you can take breaks from the intense focus and activation that anxiety often requires of you. And you can also welcome the "get the job done" aspects of anxiety when you need to take breaks from the floating and hazy aspects of confusion.

WORKING WITH ANXIETY AND CONFUSION TOGETHER

When *confusiety* is present, you may feel pulled in two directions that don't make sense: you may feel focus and motivation on one hand, yet a lack of focus or clear motivation on the other. This seemingly illogical pairing may increase your confusion and also increase your anxiety *about* your confusion! For instance, you may be preparing for a meeting or a trip, and while you know what you need to do, you may find yourself walking into a room and not knowing why you're there, putting things down in one place and not being able to find them again, or losing the entire thread of what you're doing. This can be frustrating, confusing, *and* anxiety provoking. If so, it may help to remember the third key to emotional genius: It is normal for emotions to work in pairs, groups, and clusters. In DEI, we learn how to welcome whichever emotions show up, and we work to understand how our multiple emotions might support each other (and us).

I call confusion a *masking state* because it often arises to place a kind of soft blanket over the top of fear and anxiety. If there's too much input or too many changes for your fear to keep track of, your confusion may arise to slow everything down and stop you from taking action. Or when your anxiety is overburdened by too many tasks or deadlines, your confusion may drape a gauzy blanket over you so that you can take a break and zone out. If you understand the support that confusion is trying to offer, you'll be able to reframe your response to it and relax. When you feel *confusiety*, please let yourself rest or zone out for a while if you can. There's an important reason for your confusion to be present; it's there to help you! When I'm confused, I've learned to lie down and just laze about aimlessly. It doesn't seem to matter whether I'm grounded or not; all that matters is that I take a break. Generally, after about three to five minutes of aimlessness, my confusion lifts, and I can get back to work in a different frame of mind, refreshed.

You may know that sleep is healing for your brain (your brain repairs itself, strengthens your learning, and may prune intense emotions from your memories during restorative sleep), but you may not have heard that lazing around offers many of the same healing benefits. Taking aimlessness breaks throughout the day — especially if you're in a high-demand situation at home or at work — is a great way to support yourself and give your body and your brain a rest. Doing nothing actually does a lot to heal your body and your brain, but still, we tend to value productivity over rest. This is a shame because rest is a crucial aspect of true productivity. If you can learn to see confusion as an essential part of completing your tasks and meeting your deadlines, you'll be able to take advantage of its floating and aimless nature.

This may not be true for you, but I noticed a couple of years ago that I was using television viewing or online browsing as my confusion practice, especially during intense writing deadlines. This doesn't work in the way lazing around aimlessly does. The restful lazing that brings you healing neurological benefits requires that you take a break from focus and input. There's a way that watching screens will zone you out, but there is still a lot of data and information coming at you, so it's not restful in the way that lounging and lazing around is.

During a *confusiety* break, it's important not to do things that are cognitively activating or highly focused, and as such, many of the Empathic Mindfulness practices aren't applicable. Many of them require thinking, and that's not what's needed when confusion or confusiety arise; what's needed is a complete mental rest. One practice that may be helpful for *confusiety*, however, is Resourcing. Resourcing helps you make room for more than one sensation or situation, including ones that may seem to be opposing forces. If you can focus on your anxiety or your confusion, you can gently move back and forth and use your Resourcing practice to create an open and welcoming space for both emotions. When you've cleared a space for both to coexist, you can ask each of them their internal questions.

I suggest that you ask these questions only after you have lounged around meaninglessly for a while because that's an important confusion-supporting action. After resting and Resourcing yourself (if you need to), you can ask the questions. However, since confusion can be a sign that there's simply too much going on in your life, I'll simplify the questions and make this a two-step process:

CONFUSION: *What is my intention?*

This question came to my husband, Tino Plank, in a dream back in the 1990s. He heard *Intention ends all ambiguity*, and when he woke up, he noticed that the reverse was also true: *Ambiguity ends all intention*. Since then, we've used this intention question for confusion that won't lift (after we rest, of course), and we usually find that our intentions are muddled or missing. Our anxiety was powering forward brilliantly, but it was doing work that had no real meaning. Or worse, it was doing work that would have pulled us far away from our actual intentions. When we learned to befriend our confusion and engage with it empathically, it became an important part of our self-care tool kit and a supportive partner to our anxiety.

When you've rested and have a clearer view of your intentions, you can ask the full set of questions for your *confusiety*:

CONFUSION: *What is my intention? What action should be taken?*

ANXIETY: *What brought this feeling forward? What **truly** needs to get done?*

You may find that your answer to the question about what *truly* needs to get done is quite different from the answer you would have given before your confusion arose. Often, a bout of confusion can act as an important reset button that helps you shake off old ideas that aren't really working — even though your anxiety keeps hero-ically trying to make them work. These old, unworkable ideas may require the Burning Contracts practice, which will help you let go of outworn ideas and make room for something more suitable.

The Conscious Complaining practice may also be helpful during periods of *confusiety* because it gives all of your emotions a voice. I find that I can often get to the root of an issue that's confus-ing to me if I complain consciously, out loud. I also notice that if I move into a different position, for instance, reclining on the couch or the floor, or getting up and walking around while I complain consciously, I can often shift into a new state. There's research that suggests that moving into different locations or positions can create what is called a "cognitive event boundary" for your brain.[3] Something about being in a different place can clear your perception and cognitively reset your brain, and this may create an opportunity for your confusion to shift and reconnect you to your true intentions.

As I write this book, I find that periods of confusion give rise to percolations of ideas that aren't conscious yet. Some people would call this blanking out or even writer's block, but I've learned to welcome these interruptions in my workflow. Often, when I get up and walk away from the computer, I'll remember an idea that dropped out of a chapter (easy to fix), or I'll realize that the entire structure of the book has a flaw in it (harder to fix, but thank goodness my confusion wrapped the project in a hazy fog until I saw the problem!). I also notice that when I return to writing, I can often rebuild my schedule and my to-do lists and refocus myself on what's truly important.

We tend to think of work as only those activities that are conscious, obvious, and full of effort, but there is a deeper kind of work that occurs when we're not doing anything or when our focus is misty and indistinct. These moments of not-work and not-focus are just as important to getting things done as work and focus are — and they are usually where creativity arises. If we can create a welcoming environment for our confusion and our *confusiety*, we can learn how to flow gracefully between work and rest and learn how to make room for creative impulses.

Note: If your *confusiety* doesn't shift in response to these practices, and you have regular difficulty organizing or focusing yourself (especially when anxiety is present), you may be dealing with a different and deeper situation of reduced or inconsistent focus (or possibly a traumatic situation in the past or present). An inability to focus and organize yourself may indicate some type of attention deficit or another issue that needs care; both situations may require support from your health-care professional.[4]

Sherry Olander, a DEI professional and instructor from Virginia, recalled becoming confused when her anxiety would spin problems over and over in her head. She realized that she had learned to work with her attention deficit as a young girl by repeating things over and over so that she wouldn't forget them. Her anxiety picked up this same habit, but instead of helping her remember important details, it would fixate on problems in disturbing and confusing ways. Though her anxiety was trying to help her figure things out, it felt obsessive and intrusive.

In a situation like this, Conscious Questioning probably won't help, because the anxiety doesn't need any more input. Sherry found that using Grounding (and the sadness that supports Grounding) to help her let go of things that weren't working was a more useful practice. She also found that setting her boundaries and using anger to identify what she valued helped her anxiety focus on important things, and not on every possible thing.

If you cannot focus, organize yourself, or get things done reliably, your anxiety likely needs some help. The HelpGuide website (helpguide.org) has some excellent resources for you.

PANIC AND ANXIETY: UNDERSTANDING THE DIFFERENCE BETWEEN READINESS AND SURVIVAL

Anxiety and panic are mistaken for each other *a lot*, and you can see this mistake in the term *anxiety attack*, which refers not to anxiety, but to the powerful, lifesaving emotion of panic. Panic has a different purpose than anxiety does; anxiety helps you complete your tasks and meet your deadlines, but panic literally saves your life in the face of danger. Sometimes when you're overwhelmed, your panic may arise to help your anxiety get things done, and this is likely why panic and anxiety are mistaken for each other. Identifying your panic clearly — and developing supportive practices for it — is a vital part of learning how to work with your anxiety.

Emotion	Gifts and Skills	Internal Questions
PANIC arises when you face threats to your survival. Panic gives you three lifesaving choices: *fight, flee,* or *freeze.*	Sudden energy, intense attention, absolute stillness, survival	During an emergency: *Just listen to your body.* Fight, flee, or freeze. Your body is a survival expert, and it will keep you safe. For panic that relates to past difficulties or traumas: *What has been frozen in time?* *What healing action must be taken?*
ANXIETY (*or WORRY*) is focused on **the future**. It arises to help you look ahead and identify the tasks you need to complete or the deadlines you need to meet.	Foresight, focus, task completion, procrastination alert!	*What brought this feeling forward?* *What **truly** needs to get done?*

Panic is the emotion that steps forward when your life is in danger, and it gives you the energy you need to fight, flee, or freeze so that you'll survive.[5] Sometimes, you might need panic to help you complete your work — for instance, when you are struggling with overwhelming tasks or immediate, urgent deadlines — however, you shouldn't use panic regularly in the place of anxiety. Panic contains an intensity that is appropriate when you need a lifesaving burst of energy, but it can be too much in ordinary situations. Panic is also limited in its responses, so it doesn't have the flexibility and planning skills that anxiety brings to you. If you use panic in anxiety's place, you may triage your tasks in the way a battlefield medic does; you'll only complete the most urgent tasks, while you let the ordinary ones fall away. Your powerful panic is absolutely necessary in an emergency, but it's not the ideal emotion to use to get your everyday work done. Panic can certainly help you triage in a crisis, but that's very different from prioritizing your tasks intelligently with the long-ranging vision that anxiety brings you.

Another facet of panic is related to past traumas. Panic can remain activated after an emergency if you weren't given the opportunity to down-regulate and soothe yourself, and it may reappear as intense fighting, freezing, fleeing, or flooding (being overwhelmed by intense emotions) responses, even in moments of calm and safety. This post-traumatic panic tends to partner with anxiety (*panxiety?*) for many people. Because *panxiety* often signals the presence of a still-active response to a past trauma, I'll focus on how to work with it in the next chapter.

This trauma-based connection between anxiety and panic is an important part of the reason I couldn't identify anxiety as a separate emotion before I heard Mary Lamia on the radio back in 2010. I'm a survivor of extended early childhood trauma, and I spent a lot of my early life in the necessary territory of panic. I also learned to dissociate in response to the overwhelming situations I faced as a toddler; thank you, panic! But after the abuse finally ended, I learned to keep most of my emotions at a low simmer because too much activation in any emotion would tend to bring my panic flooding back (along with memories of my abuse). Nope! No thank you! I didn't have any way to face all of that, and I didn't have access to mental health care, so I knitted together a life as best I could.

Intense anxiety can feel a lot like panic, so I avoided it completely and instead learned to respond to my anxiety when it was at a nearly undetectable whisper. I was a super do-it-aheader, and I would often complete things a year ahead of time. I see now that I was avoiding any undue activation in my anxiety, not because anxiety is bad, but because activated anxiety would engage my panic — and I didn't yet know how to work with panic without fighting (raging), flooding (becoming incapacitated by my powerful emotions), or dissociating (this was my form of fleeing plus freezing).[6] Looking back, I think that working with whisper-soft anxiety was a great solution (until I learned how to work with my panic and my dissociative tendencies), even though it meant that I was almost completely ignorant about the true nature of anxiety. Luckily, we can all learn new things about our emotions (and learn how to work with them in healthier ways) at any stage of our lives.

If you deal with *panxiety*, you may have already found practices that help you calm and soothe yourself. A simple practice that can be healing and supportive (if you need one right now) is Hands-On Grounding. Stroking and soothing your body can help your panic and your anxiety realize that you're in a safe place where they don't need to be on such high alert. Developing many ways to soothe your body is a key to working with *panxiety*, and we'll explore supportive practices and therapeutic approaches in the next chapter.

6

Attending to Panic
and Anxiety

In our DEI community, we regularly use the Conscious Questioning process to work with our anxiety, but some people noticed that there were times when it didn't help. Others noticed that their anxiety *increased* when they questioned it consciously! After many months of studying this phenomenon as a community, we learned what was going on: Panic was present alongside the anxiety. Working with the anxiety had unearthed the panic.

We learned to differentiate between what we now call *situational anxiety* (anxiety that alerts us to a situation that we can address) and what we lovingly call *panxiety* (panic and anxiety acting together and creating a continual sense of hyperactivation, apprehension, overthinking, or dread).

Emotion	Gifts and Skills	Internal Questions
PANIC arises when you face threats to your survival. Panic gives you three lifesaving choices: *fight, flee,* or *freeze.*	Sudden energy; intense attention, absolute stillness, survival	During an emergency: *Just listen to your body.* Fight, flee, or freeze. Your body is a survival expert, and it will keep you safe. For panic that relates to past difficulties or traumas: *What has been frozen in time? What healing action must be taken?*
ANXIETY (*or WORRY*) is focused on **the future**. It arises to help you look ahead and identify the tasks you need to complete or the deadlines you need to meet.	Foresight, focus, task-completion, procrastination alert!	*What brought this feeling forward?* *What **truly** needs to get done?*

Panxiety is the state that many people misname as *anxiety*. Even our medical and mental health communities misname anxiety regularly. The terms *anxiety attack* and *panic attack* are used interchangeably, and many of the so-called anxiety disorders contain or primarily involve panic (such as generalized anxiety disorder, social anxiety, separation anxiety, phobias, and so on). Certainly, each of these conditions involve anxiety because anxiety will need to keep a close eye on any situation that your panic has identified as life-threatening (fear will need to be on-task as well because you'll need heightened instincts and intuition), but none of these conditions is caused by anxiety. Anxiety is surely present, but it's not the problem. Even panic isn't the problem; panic is a vitally important and lifesaving emotion that you never want to be without. However, you do want to be able to soothe and down-regulate your panic and its Fear Family members if they're on guard and activated when no life-threatening situations are occurring.

If you deal with *panxiety* regularly, rest here for a minute and breathe gently. Feel your feet on the floor, feel your bottom and your thighs on your chair, and ask your fear to help you orient to the present moment. Reach out and feel this page or softly pat your chest, your abdomen, or your thighs with your hands. Take a break and do whatever feels right. Move around, shake your hands like you're shaking off water, get something to eat or drink, do the Hands-On Grounding practice, or lie down. Treat yourself with kindness and take care of yourself; you and your emotions have been doing *a lot* of work, and you deserve lots of soothing downtime on a regular basis.

SUPPORTIVE SUGGESTIONS FOR A
PANXIETY-PRONE BODY

Regular self-soothing and self-care are important for everyone, but they can make all the difference to people who feel *panxiety* consistently. Regular exercise, rest and relaxation, mindfulness breaks, healthy self-talk, good food, loving relationships, supportive community, quiet time, restorative sleep, bodywork, playtime, and laughter are necessary if your emotions are on high alert. Some forms of meditation can also be supportive, but be careful; people with preexisting *panxiety* can be destabilized or even hurt by some types of meditation and deep breathing practices.

Many healing approaches can have a paradoxical effect on us because we're all different and we respond differently, and meditation is no exception. Some forms of meditation attempt to change your inner state by helping you hyperfocus or detach yourself from your sense of time or space. Other forms may help you open your focus and depersonalize yourself (or dissociate). When your emotions are highly activated and sense hazards everywhere, these changes to your inner state can increase your sense of danger, and they can lead to increased anxiety, panic, or dissociation. Deep breathing practices can also activate your nervous system in the wrong way and increase your anxiety and/or your panic. None of these responses is a sign of failure on your part; these responses are a sign that these practices are wrong for you.

If you try any practice that makes your *panxiety* worse, drop it like a hot potato, no matter how many people swear by it. Better yet, let your panic fight with the practice and kick it to the curb, hard! Your emotional situation is unique, and so are you. No matter how many people tell you that something's therapeutic, if it doesn't work for you, it doesn't work. Listen to your body and pay attention to your emotions; you're their friend, and you can protect them from ideas and practices that don't work for them — or for you.

If you have access to mental health care, there are body-based therapies such as Somatic Experiencing or sensorimotor psychotherapy that can help you address the physical aspects of your panic response and restore your resilience.[1] Emotion-focused therapy can also be supportive because it explores your emotional functioning and treats your emotions as aspects of your motivation, your intelligence, and your unique responses to stressors and trauma. Cognitive behavioral approaches that help you question and reframe your intense activation can also be supportive. When panic and anxiety are in the driver's seat, they can get themselves into a feedback loop where your anxiety will search for upcoming hazards, and your panic will prepare to fight, flee, or freeze (etc.). In this highly activated state, your anxiety may ramp up even more and begin to expect danger everywhere (and of course, your panic will respond, because it has to!). Somatic, emotion-focused, and cognitive therapies can help you work with these responses and calm yourself so that you can gently pause the feedback loop or stop the loop from forming in the first place.

If you can't access mental health care, there are a lot of things you can do to help yourself. The four keys to emotional genius from chapter 1 (see page 22) are pivotal in a mixed-emotion situation like this because your anxiety and your panic need you to engage with them lovingly, perceptively, and empathically. If you don't understand what these two emotions are trying to do for you and for each other, you'll probably view and experience them as a problem, a disorder, or a disaster. And you'll react accordingly, probably with more panic.

But these emotions are not problems; they have jobs to do. Panic and anxiety can feel overwhelming, but they need a friend when they're stuck in a feedback loop, and they need your help. They need to be unvalenced so that you can respond to them instead of reacting to them. They need to be identified precisely (see the Emotional Vocabulary Lists in chapter 2) so that you can gauge their level of activation. They need to be welcomed in their paired-up state because it's normal for emotions to work together. And they need to be listened to empathically and channeled intentionally so that they can contribute their gifts and intelligence to you and then recede until you need them again.

WORKING WITH ANXIETY AND PANIC TOGETHER

When *panxiety* is present, you may experience a highly activated state that doesn't help you get things done. You may feel hyperfocused or completely unfocused. You may feel intense activation, or you may feel exhausted and worn out. You may imagine hazards, tragedies, and terrible outcomes (which may scare you and increase your panic), or you may lose your ability to think at all. Pay attention if you experience any lack of focus or an inability to think clearly. Is confusion trying to help you take a time-out? Remember that confusion will arise when there's too much activation and too much input; confusion shows up to help you. Skip back to the confusion section if your confusion is trying to give you a break from your *panxiety* (is this *panfusiety*?).

When *panxiety* is present, you may also feel as if you're incapable or that you always do everything wrong, so why even try? This could signal the presence of other emotions: guilt and shame if you experience self-doubt or self-loathing, and depression if you lose your energy or your interest.

First things first: What is your panic responding to? Is there a current emergency? Look around: Are you in danger? If so, it's time to act quickly and save your life by working directly with your panic:

PANIC (during an emergency): *Just listen to your body. Don't think, just react: fight, flee, or freeze. Your body is a survival expert, and it will keep you safe.*

If you look around yourself and find no immediate danger, then it's time for a different approach and a different set of questions for your nonurgent form of panic. Your anxiety is likely bringing your attention to your panic for important reasons. Remember that your anxiety doesn't just look outside you and toward the future to help you get things done; it also searches inside you to find anything that might get in the way of your ability to succeed.

When *panxiety* is present, your anxiety may be highlighting a form of panic that relates to the past. This panic might relate to something dangerous that happened in the past, yet it feels similar to something your anxiety is working on today. Or this panic might be a remnant of a past trauma (which you may not remember clearly) that's still activated for some reason and may obstruct your ability to get things done in the present day.

When your anxiety highlights panic that's focused in the past, it's important to ground and focus yourself if you can. The Grounding and Focusing practice relies on the soothing gifts of sadness and the orienting gifts of fear to help you calm your body, release your tension, and locate yourself in the present moment. Breathe in gently and breathe out and down to soothe yourself. If you have a private space, place your hands on your head and gently run your hands all the way down your body. As you lean forward to run your hands down your thighs and your calves, you may want to lower your head down and just hang for a few seconds. Thank your sadness and fear, and when you feel settled, you can ask the first part of the anxiety question:

ANXIETY: *What brought this feeling forward?*

If this past-focused panic relates to a dangerous situation or event that has bearing on your current situation, take some time to study what happened. The Conscious Questioning practice may help you organize your concerns. You can use the questions to learn more about why your anxiety is highlighting this panic and create a plan to move forward (or ask for support) now that you recall this past danger that could trip you up today. This kind of awareness is uncomfortable, but it's often necessary, especially when you're trying to create something new, move forward into unknown territory, or address a longstanding problem that involves many preexisting issues.

As a simple example, imagine that you're planning a trip. You and your anxiety are humming along, organizing all of your ideas and gathering supplies, and suddenly, your anxiety ramps up into a panicky state. In a split second, your trip takes on a haunted feel, and the whole project fills you with dread. You look around yourself to see if there's an emergency, but everything's fine, so you don't need to fight, flee, or freeze. You suspect that this panic relates to the past. You slow down, ground and focus yourself if you can, and ask your anxiety: *What brought this feeling forward?*

Perhaps you remember a time when a trip was cut short by a natural disaster or by an injury or illness. Knowing this, you can use the Conscious Questioning practice to devise a plan to avoid that kind of trouble this time — or perhaps to prepare ahead for it so that you're not taken by surprise. If you need support, you can talk things through with a friend or loved one and explore what your *panxiety* is trying to alert you to. Sometimes it takes a while to figure out what's going on because if this situation were easy to recall, you would have thought of it already. This kind of *panxiety* usually points to important information that's been forgotten for some reason, so you may need to feel into the situation for a while.

Conscious Complaining may also help because it's a stream-of-consciousness practice that allows all of your emotions to have a voice. Sometimes you need to speak out loud to find out what you already know. The Burning Contracts practice can also be helpful because exploring the contract you've created in regard to this trip (or the destination or what you'll do there or whom you'll be with, and so on) may help you zero in on the problem. The empathic approach to this kind of *panxiety* is to use your skills to feel into the source of the dread or unease so that you can identify it and create options for yourself if anything like it should happen again. This kind of *panxiety* arises to help you develop your skills and resources for troubles and calamities that have occurred or may be likely to occur. This *panxiety* takes problems seriously and helps you prepare as best you can for the future. Thank you, *panxiety*.

IF YOUR PANXIETY RELATES TO A TRAUMA THAT IS STILL ACTIVATED

If you feel into the nonurgent panic that arises alongside your anxiety and ask yourself what brought this feeling forward, you may sense a feeling of dread or activation that doesn't track to anything relevant to your current situation. Nothing around you is dangerous, so you don't need to fight, flee, or freeze. The panicky feeling also doesn't contribute any specific information to help you complete your tasks or meet your deadlines.

In this situation, your *panxiety* may be revisiting a past trauma that's still activated. For instance, if you were in a car accident, and you haven't been able to calm and soothe all of your panic-based activation, you may still have a strong startle response when you hear loud noises. You may avoid the area where the accident occurred, you may dread driving, or you may experience other trauma-related responses. The trauma occurred in the past, but it's carrying forward into your present-day behavior. This is a simple example of a still-activated traumatic response. Of course, these responses can be much more complex. Mine were, and there were many that I couldn't track to any specific memory or event. If you have *panxiety* responses that don't make sense, somatic healing approaches such as Somatic Experiencing can help you access these body-based responses, resolve your hyperactivation, and settle your system.

To my eye, trauma-related *panxiety* is the form that's most often mistaken for anxiety. This is the misnamed anxiety attack. It's the misnamed anxiety disorder. This is an understandable mistake for people who don't understand the value of mixed emotions because anxiety is certainly involved in this response; however, the main emotion here is panic. This is also post-traumatic stress disorder (PTSD), but I don't support the use of that term because I challenge the idea that trauma-related responses like these are disordered. They can certainly feel out of place, destabilizing, or frightening, and they can lead us to respond in unusual or unhealthy ways to seemingly normal situations. However, if a traumatic response is still activated because it has not been down-regulated, resolved, or integrated, then it's important for your emotional system and your anxiety to highlight it. I call this a post-traumatic *response* rather than a disorder because it's normal to respond strongly to trauma, and it's normal to need support to deal with and down-regulate from it.

Your *panxiety* may also be related to an ongoing situation of social inequality, illness, poverty, or a lack of safety. Remember that your social insight may need to be pitched at a higher frequency when your social situation is unwelcoming, unhealthy, or unsafe. This means that your fear, your anxiety, and your panic may need to be on constant watch. The *panxiety* you experience in unequal situations certainly relates to your past experiences, but it also relates to the present and the future. Your *panxiety* will need to look out for you every day; however, living in a hyperactivated state with these two emotions can wear you out.

The Anxioneers and I have seen that when a past trauma is still activated, and panic is still working on basic survival, anxiety will continually bring the situation to our awareness. If you recall my avoidance of anything but the subtlest activations of anxiety, you may see that I was also avoiding panic and the awareness of my still-active traumatic responses. I survived many years of sexual and emotional abuse in early childhood, and I was persistently dissociated; it was lovely to float above the world and not really be affected by anything. Anxiety's job, which is to make sure that I was prepared and resourced, was hindered by my panic-based responses. Therefore, every time I allowed anxiety to rise above a whisper (and I didn't do that very often!), it would bring panic with it. Of course, I shut it down. Of course!

When feelings of dread, activation, or panic arise alongside your anxiety, you may be filled with energy but unable to focus or ground yourself. You may be ready to fight, flee, or freeze but be unable to identify the threat (or you may sense threat everywhere and not know where to look or what to do first). Your anxiety may also increase because so much uncertainty and activation are present. Your anxiety wants to help you prepare, but because this post-traumatic panic relates to the past, there may be no clear plan or direction to help your anxiety orient itself. In response, you may spin out and lose your focus — or you may become super-functional in the midst of all of this activation and uncertainty (many survivors of childhood trauma become heroic caretakers in their troubled early lives and may seek out heroic caretaker relationships or jobs later in life). You may also reach toward whatever soothing practices you've developed, such as eating, using mood-altering substances, distracting yourself, or engaging with your addiction of choice. Or like me, you may dissociate and leave the scene.

Clearly, when your *panxiety* is pointing toward a still-active trauma, you'll need social support, therapy, and possibly medication to calm your hyperactivated system, plus other forms of support that are outside the scope of this book. You can use the many practices in this book and create a caring emotional environment for yourself and your *panxiety*, but this likely won't be enough. It's important to take *panxiety* that relates to still-active trauma seriously. You've been through something intense. Your system is still being affected by it. Your anxiety, your panic, and your entire emotional system need loving and significant support.

Anxioneer Sarah Alexander from Oregon is a DEI professional and clinical social worker who works with *panxiety* in her practice, and she helped us see how important the questioning process is for this kind of *panxiety*. As a reminder, these are the questions for nonurgent panic:

PANIC (that relates to past difficulties or traumas): *What has been frozen in time? What healing action must be taken?*

Sarah would probably underline, italicize, and bold the word *healing* in the second question because *panxiety* has so much energy that you could complete almost any task in the world or run around in a thousand different directions (or freeze and dissociate). But would any of these actions be *healing*? Would they address your still-activated panic response? Would they soothe your body? Would they help you ground yourself? Would they help you heal? Or would they just help you survive?

Survival is magnificent, and it's the gift of your brilliant panic, but after survival should come understanding, reintegration, and healing. Asking yourself what healing action must be taken — among the hundreds of actions that you might take — can help you address what's actually going on inside your *panxiety* response. Orienting yourself toward healing actions means intentionally supporting your body and listening to your emotions rather than suppressing, overusing, or running away from them. When you're having a *panxiety* response, your panic and your anxiety need your loving help. They need you to take the lead and choose actions that will bring them peace and healing. They need support.

HEALING VERSUS DUBIOUS ACTIONS FOR ATTENDING TO YOUR PANIC

The following table offers some suggestions for healing actions and contrasts them with dubious actions that will get *something* done but won't likely lead to healing.

Healing Actions	Dubious Actions
Grounding and soothing yourself	Ignoring your body and your needs
Working lovingly with your *panxiety*	Valencing your *panxiety* as negative
Resting and taking downtime	Zoning out in front of the TV or computer
Finding trauma-informed therapy	Toughing it out and suffering alone
Reaching out for loving support	Pushing people away
Organizing your tasks mindfully with the help of your grounded anxiety	Working yourself far too hard, failing your tasks, or missing your deadlines

Healing Actions	Dubious Actions
Eating nourishing food on a regular schedule	Overeating to numb yourself, obsessing over the perfect diet, undereating, or forgetting to eat
Developing a regular and healthy movement practice	Becoming immobile or using exercise to distract yourself, burn off your panic, or exhaust yourself
Practicing Resourcing and Rejuvenation	Using substances, behaviors, or dissociation to achieve a sense of peace, relief, or happiness
Practicing Conscious Complaining	Complaining unconsciously or silencing yourself because no one will listen anyway
Practicing Burning Contracts	Reinforcing old contracts by refusing to explore or challenge them
Practicing Defining Your Boundary	Letting circumstances or other people set your boundaries for you
Finding a supportive community of people who are working on similar challenges	Isolating yourself or convincing yourself that healing isn't possible
Choosing healthy relationship partners who are safe, soothing, and loving	Choosing unavailable or unstable partners who activate your panic response

As a trauma survivor, I did everything in the dubious column for decades, and *surprise*, I didn't heal anything. Instead, my life became less stable and more dangerous. Now that I've resolved those traumas (with the help of my *panxiety* responses and the practices in this book), I don't need to dissociate or do anything in the dubious column. When any level of *panxiety* arises in me today, I have many choices and a ton of support from my emotions. Together, my emotions and I can usually resolve the still-activated trauma in a few hours or days. I'm not telling you this so you'll think I'm magical; I want you to know that you can go through hell and find a way out, thanks to the genius and healing that emotions bring to all of us. If you need more support right now, the Somatic Experiencing approach is very helpful, and the HelpGuide website (helpguide.org) has excellent free information on trauma healing.

This healing process took me a while because I was deeply habituated to the dubious actions in the preceding table. I had trained myself over many decades to be a master of dissociation, ungroundedness, boundary impairment, distraction, isolation, and rigidity. Retraining myself to seek healing actions in response to my panic took months (or even years, depending on the behavior), but it worked. Using the DEI concepts and practices in this book, I slowly retrained myself to identify and choose integration, groundedness, healthy boundaries, clear focus, emotional honesty and awareness, intentional self-care, effective and worthwhile behaviors, loving relationships with healthy people, caring community, laughter, and wholeness.

This self-retraining required consistent and deliberate repetitions of many healing actions (not to mention fierce hope and determination). I also needed to identify and reduce any *panxiety*-generating activities (watching TV news, being on social media, watching violent or scary dramas, and so on) from my life while I was healing. I isolated myself during this healing process, but I wasn't alone. My emotions supported me, kept me company, strengthened me, made me laugh, and helped me maintain my unfamiliar new behaviors until they became easier. My Empathic Mindfulness practices, and especially Burning Contracts and Rejuvenation, helped me walk away from my old traumatic training and head toward something new.

The Anxioneers have many helpful ideas about how to work with *panxiety* in the early days when it can still be in a powerful feedback loop. Jennifer Asdorian, a DEI professional from Washington, DC, suggests Resourcing when *panxiety* won't calm down because it helps people know that they have inner resources even when *panxiety* is very active. Jeanette Brynn, a DEI professional from the state of Washington, notices that *panxiety* can turn on suddenly, almost like a switch, and that physical self-soothing practices such as the Hands-On Grounding practice can help with down-regulation. Jennifer Nate, a DEI professional from Alberta, Canada, finds that increasing the felt sense of grounding in the Grounding and Focusing practice can help people feel that they're releasing their excess activation into the ground. When you're dealing with *panxiety* and the traumatic residue it contains, many self-soothing practices are necessary.

Traumas that are still activated need to be resolved and healed, and anxiety does us a huge favor by bringing them to our awareness. Our job as loving and empathic friends to our emotions is to take post-traumatic panic seriously and reach out for the help and healing we need. Thank you, anxiety, panic, and *panxiety*. You are intense emotions, my friends, but you don't cause the traumas; you arise to help us heal them. Thank you.

In the next chapter, we'll explore the important relationship between your anger and your anxiety. These two emotions help you identify work that's important and meaningful to you, and they can help you set boundaries around your work. However, anger and anxiety are activating emotions, and when they arise together, you may feel agitated or lose your focus (mostly due to the ways we've all learned to treat anger). We'll explore new ways to approach anger so that you can work efficiently on tasks and projects that have meaning and value for you.

7

Setting Clear Boundaries with Anger and Anxiety

A nger and anxiety are partners that help you get important things done, but because both of these emotions are valenced negatively, many people avoid them and don't learn how they work. Many of us can only recognize anger when it rises to an intense state like rage, so we tend to misidentify anger as a forceful or even violent emotion. That's a big mistake. People can certainly do damage with their anger, but that's not anger's fault. The fault lies with our very poor training about emotions, and about anger in particular. Anger is not about violence; at its core, anger is about helping you set clear boundaries around what you value.

Emotion	Gifts and Skills	Internal Questions
ANGER arises when your self-image, behaviors, values, or interpersonal boundaries are challenged — or when you see them challenged in someone else.	Honor, certainty, healthy self-esteem, proper boundaries, healthy detachment, protection of yourself and others	*What do I value?* *What must be protected and restored?*
ANXIETY (*or WORRY*) is focused on **the future**. It arises to help you look ahead and identify the tasks you need to complete and the deadlines you need to meet.	Foresight, focus, task completion, procrastination alert!	*What brought this feeling forward?* *What **truly** needs to get done?*

Each of the four keys to emotional genius from chapter 1 (see page 22) will help you approach your anger in a workable way. Certainly, you want to unvalence this vital emotion because it helps you set boundaries around yourself and things that are vitally important to you, and it helps you detach in healthy ways from things that aren't important. If you don't have enough healthy anger, you won't set proper boundaries, you won't be able to identify or protect what's important to you, and you may not be able to detach yourself from things that have no value. If you don't know how to welcome your anger, your anxiety will probably be overloaded with tasks and projects that have no real meaning or benefit for you.

Understanding that anger arises at many different levels of intensity is also important because if you only identify anger when it's forceful, you may not learn how to recognize or work with it at subtler levels of activation. Your emotional vocabulary is vital to helping you become aware of your soft and subtle levels of anger. For instance, can you identify your anger when it appears as certainty, detachment, displeasure, indifference, or frustration? Anger is not merely rage; anger has many facets.

Knowing about mixed emotions is also key to working with anger. Many people mistakenly see anger as a "secondhand" emotion because they notice that anger often arises when people are sad, afraid, anxious, depressed, and so forth. You may have noticed this when you're cranky or snappish when a deadline is looming, or when you're unable to express emotions in public (such as fear or sadness) and your anger steps forward to protect you. In these instances, your anger isn't out of place, and it isn't behaving incorrectly; it's doing what anger is supposed to do, which is setting boundaries for you. Knowing this, you can learn to welcome and work with your anger appropriately; it arises to help you set clear boundaries, and you can set them in many ways. You have choices with your anger, and with all of your emotions.

Channeling your anger by recognizing it, listening to it, and asking its questions will help you uncover its genius. When you can welcome your anger's gifts and intelligence, you can learn how to identify what's important to you and develop healthy self-esteem that's based on your internal sense of values and integrity. Your well-channeled anger can help you set clear boundaries, respect them in others, and restore your sense of self when you're challenged.

Your anger is a vital partner to your anxiety (*angerxiety?*) because it helps you identify what's important and what's not. If your anger isn't present when you agree to tasks or projects, you may take on far too much because you can't say no. Or you may agree to an unworkable deadline because you don't know how to speak up and negotiate a better schedule. Your anger can protect you from taking on inappropriate or meaningless responsibilities, which means that it can protect your anxiety from busywork or overwork. The DEI motto for anxiety that I shared in chapter 4, "There's always enough time for every important thing," uses *angerxiety* to set boundaries not just in regard to time, but also in regard to what's truly important. This motto can remind you that you have choices and the ability to make decisions even when you're intensely busy.

When your anger works well with its fellow emotions, it will protect them so that they can do their own jobs successfully. To help your anger work well, you can use the Defining Your Boundary practice to become aware of where you begin and end. This practice (along with Grounding and Focusing and Conscious Complaining) will help you work with your anger mindfully and set your boundaries regularly so that your anger won't have to ramp up into rage unless it's absolutely necessary. You need your anger every day, and in pretty much every situation you face, so learning these practices will help your anger respond at many different levels of activation instead of coming on too strong or disappearing entirely.

Your anxiety requires your anger's support and clarity so that its work will be appropriate to your true needs (and the true needs of your friends, family, and colleagues if your tasks and projects involve others).

WORKING WITH ANXIETY AND ANGER TOGETHER

When your anger and your anxiety work well together, you'll be able to set clear and peaceful boundaries with the help of your anger, and you'll be able to prepare yourself, gather your resources, and complete your tasks and projects with the help of your anxiety. But if you don't have the emotional skills you need to work with these two emotions, you might overexpress your anger and lash out at people (or set harsh boundaries), or you might repress your anger and fail to set any boundaries at all. You might also overexpress your anxiety and spin yourself out, or you might suppress your anxiety in any way you can. When you don't have the skills you need to work with your emotions (especially mixed emotions), they can feel miserable, irrational, or out of control. They're not, of course, but they can feel that way.

The key to working with your *angerxiety* is to attend to your anger first. Anger sets boundaries and helps you understand what you value, so its wisdom can lead you to change, renegotiate, or cancel the work that your anxiety is doing. When your *angerxiety* is present, it's not time to barrel ahead with your tasks and projects, because something is clearly amiss. It's time to engage with your anger empathically.

If your *angerxiety* is highly activated, you may need to ground and focus yourself first and then check on your boundary. Notice what happens to your sense of personal space when you feel highly activated. If your boundary changes or disappears, it may be helpful to perform the Hands-On Grounding practice and then set your boundaries by describing them with your hands. You can also use your breath to down-regulate yourself: breathe in through your nose and breathe out with a sigh to help soothe yourself. If you still feel too activated, it may help to use the Conscious Complaining practice and move or walk around as you do so. You may find that your *angerxiety* requires a move- ment practice and a chance to say whatever you need to say before you can focus on the anger questions:

ANGER: *What do I value? What must be protected and restored?*

Asking these questions in the middle of a project can be jarring, which is why many of us repress the anger part of our *angerxiety*. These questions might make us realize that we don't value the project and that what we want to protect and restore is our own time and energy. Because we might not want to face this inconvenient truth, we may instead focus solely on our anxiety, work tirelessly, and get things finished already. There's a certain logic to that because if you start asking yourself what you value every time you start a task or project, you might never finish any of your tedious-but-necessary chores.

But if you can ask yourself these anger questions in the middle of a task, you'll have important information for the next tasks and projects you do. We learn by doing, and by making mistakes, so it's okay to discover that you don't value what you're doing — or that you agreed to something that can't work for you. You may also discover that you *do* value this work but that you're uncomfortable with a specific aspect of it. Asking these questions is never a bad idea, even if your answers disrupt your anxiety's forward progress. As we learned from *confusiety*, it's often important to slow down your anxiety and reassess what you're doing. Confusion can do that for you, as can anger and depression (see chapter 9).

When you have some clarity about what's meaningful and valuable to you, you can then ask your anxiety questions:

ANXIETY: *What brought this feeling forward? What **truly** needs to get done?*

Your ideas about what *truly* needs to get done may change when your *angerxiety* is present, and you may discover a new, internally generated motivation. You may connect with what's important to you, you may realize that you need to make changes in your work or your relationships, and you may discover that agreeing to things that don't serve you is a theme in your life (burn that contract!). Your *angerxiety* can upload this new information and help you organize a new approach to your work, your responsibilities, and your relationships.

IF YOUR ANGER RARELY SUPPORTS YOUR ANXIETY

If you don't know how to set clear boundaries around tasks and projects — if you don't have *enough* anger — you may find yourself agreeing to do things you don't have time for, don't enjoy, or cannot complete. Many women tend to do this because they want to be seen as friendly, and in the spiritual community I grew up in (where anger was heavily valenced and exiled), people agreed to a lot of things that they didn't actually care about or want to do. I noticed that without their anger, these people either lost their connection to themselves or were filled with an inner seething that they couldn't manage or even admit to. Exiling anger seems like a good idea, but in practice, it doesn't work at all. Anger is a vitally important emotion, and you can't function properly without it. Your anxiety can't function well without it either.

You may also agree to do too many things because you're excited by countless ideas and opportunities that you can't prioritize. This lack of discernment can mean that your anxiety has far too much to do, and you may find yourself up-regulating into panic simply because you need the boost of energy that panic provides. If you can't say no, and you can't set boundaries around what you can and cannot do, your anxiety may be overworked most of the time. In addition to needing the support of your panic, your overworked anxiety may also need help from your confusion (see chapter 5), your shame (see chapter 8), or your depression (see chapter 9) just to make it through the day. Your anxiety will need a great deal of support from its fellow emotions if you can't set boundaries.

But there's a twist here: many people see (or were taught to see) boundary setting as a form of unkindness or rudeness; it's not *nice*. If you've agreed to this rule, your shame and your anxiety may be activated when you try to set any kind of boundary (see the next chapter for support). Your shame may arise because you're breaking the terms of your agreement about boundaries (burn that contract!), but your anxiety may also arise because your future as a nice person is in doubt. If you hold to this rule very strongly, your panic might also arise because challenging this rule may feel life-threatening. It's a lot to deal with! The Burning Contracts practice is a vital part of challenging this rule and getting your self-determination back.

But don't blame yourself. Many of us carry this no-boundaries rule around in some form or fashion. Girls and women tend to be socialized to be nice, and setting boundaries is not often seen as nice. Children in troubled homes may also learn that setting boundaries invites punishment or abuse, while people in marginalized communities may learn that their anger is completely unwelcome in the dominant culture. There are many reasons for us *not* to set boundaries.

LEARNING TO SET BOUNDARIES AROUND TASKS AND DEADLINES

I developed the Defining Your Boundary practice as a visualization and body-based practice because I noticed that many people don't know how to embody boundaries or even imagine how to set them; it's an unknown language. They have very little life experience of setting clear boundaries, so it doesn't work to teach them boundary-setting sentences like, "No, I prefer not to do it that way," or "That deadline is too close for me; let's extend it." I find that many people have to learn to set firm and loving boundaries from the ground up: with their bodies and imaginations first. After they have a bodily experience of boundaries, then they can more easily set boundaries with their words and behaviors. It's a developmental process in a culture that valences anger severely and only allows a few people at the top to set boundaries (that are often unloving). We don't have a lot of role models or clear examples of good boundary setting, so it's understandable that many of us don't know how to set effective boundaries. It takes practice.

Defining Your Boundary and Burning Contracts are important parts of this practice, and so is asking yourself the anger questions every time you're asked to take on a task or a project. You may not be able to say no or do any form of negotiation right out of the gate, so be kind to yourself. Learning to set boundaries takes practice and many small steps, but you can develop your skills by asking yourself these questions:

ANGER: *What do I value? What must be protected and restored?*

First, notice what you value. Is it your time? Your peace and quiet? Your position as a nice person? Your position as someone who can always be depended on, no matter what? Your sense of importance and value? Your boundless curiosity and enthusiasm? Your safety in your social world? How does *not* setting boundaries serve you, and how does it affect your anxiety? Then you can ask the anxiety questions:

ANXIETY: *What brought this feeling forward? What **truly** needs to get done?*

You may continue to obey the rule that you're not allowed to set boundaries, and you may continue to take on too much in order to be seen as nice, enthusiastic, or dependable. But you will at least have asked yourself what you value. You will at least have invited the healing influence of anger into your life. And in so doing, you will have initiated a change in a behavior that may have served you in the past but isn't serving you any longer.

This exploratory process can help you understand yourself more clearly and make changes that support your values and your needs. It may take a while, and you'll certainly slip up, because setting boundaries is an alien behavior for many people. But you will be able to shift this behavior with the help of your emotions. I speak to you as a person who had no boundaries at all and who was pushed through life like a leaf on the wind. After burning endless contracts and learning to build my boundaries with sheer hope and determination, I was able to make a healthy home for my anger, my anxiety, and all of my emotions — and for myself too.

It's work, but it's good work if you can get it.

In the next chapter, we'll explore the important relationship between your guilt and shame and your anxiety. These emotions help you get your work done properly and on time, but they can feel punishing if you don't know why they've joined forces. We'll explore new ways to think about guilt and shame so that you can work efficiently and feel appropriately proud of yourself.

8

Doing Your Best Work
with Shame and Anxiety

There's a special relationship between your task-focused anxiety and your behavior-focused shame, and your life can become much more peaceful and efficient if you learn how to work well with both emotions. Shame is an important part of getting your work done properly, even though its presence can be challenging or painful at times.

Emotion	Gifts and Skills	Internal Questions
SHAME arises to make sure that you don't hurt, embarrass, or dehumanize yourself or others.	Integrity, self-respect, making amends, behavioral guidelines, behavioral change	*Who has been hurt?* *What must be made right?*
ANXIETY (*or WORRY*) is focused on **the future**. It arises to help you look ahead and identify the tasks you need to complete or the deadlines you need to meet.	Foresight, focus, task completion, procrastination alert!	*What brought this feeling forward?* *What **truly** needs to get done?*

I've stopped using the term *guilt/shame* in this chapter for good reason. In my book *The Language of Emotions*, I make a case for moving the concept of guilt out of the way so that we can focus on the emotion of shame properly. I don't need you to erase the word *guilt* from your vocabulary, and I know that my approach is unusual, but it helps me work with shame more effectively.

Quickly stated, many people believe that guilt is a lighter and more manageable emotion than shame because guilt allegedly arises when you *did* something wrong, while shame allegedly arises when you *are* something wrong. I don't agree. I see guilt as a fact: you're either guilty because you did something, or you're not guilty because you didn't. *Shame* is the emotion you feel in response to your guilt, whether it's for wrongdoing or "wrong being." To my empathic eye, what people call guilt is actually shame about something they did, while what they call shame is shame about something they are.

Many people separate guilt from shame because they assume that feeling ashamed about what you are is not survivable. I could not disagree more strenuously. Working with shame about what you are (or what you have become) is something people all over the world and all throughout history have done magnificently. This powerful work of shame is the work of transformation and soul-making, profound poetry, epic dramas, deep ecology, and the evolution of human nature itself. Feeling shame about what you are can be excruciating, but it is often a necessary pain. Certainly, there are aspects of shame that need to be managed skillfully, such as shaming that is used as a control tactic by authority figures, peers, or the media — but shame itself is a vital and essential emotion. Burning Contracts is a specific practice for shame, and it works when you feel shame about something you did, something you are, or something you've been coerced or manipulated into feeling ashamed of (such as shame about unchangeable aspects of your core self).

Shame keeps a close eye on your behavior and your agreements, and it makes sure that you don't disrespect yourself or others. Shame keeps you upright, ethical, and accountable for your thoughts, ideas, and actions. If you've *done* something wrong, your shame should arise to help you apologize, make amends, and learn to do better next time. If you've *become* something wrong, your shame should arise to help you apologize, change your behavior and your approach, make amends, and evolve as a person. And if you've *been shamed* or told that essential parts of you are broken or unacceptable (such as your body, your skin color, your intelligence, your sexuality, your emotions, your ancestry, or any other core part of you), your shame may upload those abusive shaming messages. Hopefully, your anger will arise in response to these abusive messages and set boundaries around them, but in many cases, it won't be able to.

Though working with abusive shaming messages is outside the scope of this book on anxiety, it's important to understand when your shame and anxiety are responding to abuse. For instance, if your shame reminds you to take care of yourself and eat a good breakfast because you tend to jump right into your work and forget to eat (hello, anxiety), that's a healthy shame response, even though it may feel annoying to be slowed down in the morning. But if your anxiety ramps up when you even *think* about food, and your shame jumps in with endless rules about perfect foods, evil foods, and strict rules about how your body needs to look or no one will ever love you — yikes! You're dealing with abuse.

When your shame is acting in service to abusive messages, it will feel and be abusive — but that's not the fault of shame. That's not shame's true nature. When your shame has ingested the abusive messages you've agreed to (or been coerced into), it's simply doing its job, which is to keep a close eye on your behavior and hold you to the ethics and morals you've agreed to (or been shamed into accepting). The healing practice is not to erase your shame; it's to get to the root of any abusive messages or agreements and change them into something worthwhile that you and your shame can be proud of upholding. Therapy can certainly help you heal from abuse, and there are also several supportive shame practices in DEI (beyond Burning Contracts).[1] Each of these practices recruits the boundary-setting genius of anger to help you separate yourself from abuse.

Shame is a powerful emotion because it needs to be; its work is crucial for your social survival and the health of your relationships. Your sense of shame should develop in infancy, and if it doesn't, you won't develop empathy properly because you won't have a clear sense of your effect on others or how to relate to them.[2] Shame monitors your behavior and makes sure that you act in ethical, caring, and respectful ways.

The healing work with shame is to make sure that the messages and agreements it has uploaded are livable, appropriate, and worthy of you and the people you care about. If they're not, the Burning Contracts practice can help you become aware of those unhealthy or abusive agreements so that you can withdraw your consent from them.

Shame may feel troubling or even overwhelming at times, but at its heart it is a magnificent and essential emotion. Shame helps you understand and manage your behavior, empathize well, and care about (and for) yourself, your relationships, and the world. You cannot function properly without your shame.

Your shame will regularly join with your anxiety (*shmanxiety?*) to help you get things done and meet your deadlines and responsibilities successfully.[3] *Shmanxiety* is a vital part of doing your best work, and when your shame and anxiety work well together, they'll keep you on task, on time, skillful, and reliable.

WORKING WITH ANXIETY AND SHAME TOGETHER

Your ability to unvalence emotions is a crucial skill in the area of *shmanxiety* because both shame and anxiety tend to be seen as behavioral problems instead of emotions. Many people treat shame and anxiety as useless or worthless, or they outright hate them. Because of this, many of us have learned to react to our *shmanxiety* as if it is a threat or a character flaw. It's easy to fall back into valencing when these emotions arise because they're both powerful in their own ways, and they hold us to high standards that can feel unsettling or, in the case of abusive shaming messages, excruciating. And when these two emotions are unbalanced, they can feel utterly miserable.

But if you react to your *shmanxiety* as negative, antisocial, or unwanted, you'll likely call forth other emotions such as fear, panic, depression, grief, more shame, anger, or more anxiety. Then, you'll have a crowd of emotions to deal with instead of the two that were actually relevant. Valencing is always a problem, but in the territory of powerful mixed emotions like *shmanxiety*, valencing can throw you into a situation of emotional overload that is completely unnecessary. The key with mixed emotions and powerful emotions is to ground and focus yourself, welcome them, engage with them empathically, and befriend them; they have gifts and guidance for you.

Your anxiety focuses on how and when you get things done. It's an important part of how you perform and behave, which means that your shame will often be involved with it. Shame keeps a close watch on your behavior to make sure that you're living up to your agreements, your morals, and your ethics. Are you on time? Do you complete your work? Do you attend to every detail? Are you a successful procrastinator who gets projects in on time? Can people rely on you? Can you rely on yourself? Anxiety certainly brings you the focus and energy you need to get things done, but shame brings you the *reason* to get things done: do you care about performing well and supporting other people with your work? Do you care about how you're seen? Do you care that your work ethic can signal your level of respect or love for other people? Anxiety helps you get your work done, but shame helps you care enough to do your work well and on time.

Having said that, *shmanxiety* that is based on abuse or trauma can spin you in a hundred different directions so that you not only *can't* get your work done but you feel terrible about whatever you managed to complete. These two emotions can be a double whammy if their marching orders come from the past, from unresolved trauma, or from abuse. And if you have any difficulties with attention or focusing, your anxiety may work overtime to help you complete tasks that continually slip away from you — which would then bring your shame forward because you have failed to complete your work. It's easy to understand why people valence these emotions as negative when so much trouble seems to come from them. However, my *shmanxiety* tells me that it's important for you to observe situations in which these linked emotions work beautifully together so that you can recognize their gifts.

Let's look at a *shmanxiety* situation of fooling around when you're faced with difficult and complex tasks. You're not confused or tired, and you're not feeling panic; instead, you're pretending that you can get away with avoiding your work. Your shame and anxiety may wake you up too early one morning with a sense of activation, concern, or a feeling of self-recrimination or disappointment with yourself. If you can ask yourself the shame questions, you'll likely be able to address what's happening.

Before you do, it may help you to ground and focus yourself so that you can let go of any tension and focus yourself on the situation. The Defining Your Boundary practice can also help you create clear separations between your internal sense of what's right and the often-inappropriate shaming messages of the outside world. When you feel ready, you can ask the shame questions first:

SHAME: *Who has been hurt? What must be made right?*

The hurt party might be you; you may be hurting yourself in the long run by fooling around. The hurt party might be people who rely on you to complete your tasks. When your shame arises, it does so to right a wrong. The empathic approach to shame is to listen and accept that you've done something wrong. Don't make excuses, don't blame others, and don't run away. Take note of the wrong and make it right. This can be a painful process, but it can also be a quick one if you catch your shame when it's at a soft level and respond to it as soon as possible. It's helpful to learn how to identify powerful emotions when they're at their soft and subtle levels of activation. With shame, this might mean attending to it when you feel the soft shame states of awkward, hesitant, or flustered (see the Emotional Vocabulary Lists in chapter 2 for examples of soft emotional states in each emotional category). For anxiety, this might mean attending to it when you feel alert, fidgety, or energized.

When you've identified the wrong (you've been fooling around and avoiding your work) and you've made it right (you've made a plan to get back to work and make amends to anyone you've let down), you can then ask the anxiety questions:

ANXIETY: *What brought this feeling forward? What **truly** needs to get done?*

It's likely that your fooling around brought this feeling forward, and now that you're aware of it and ready to work, you can focus on what needs to get done. When you attend to your *shmanxiety* early in its trajectory, it's a pretty easy mixed emotion to work with. The key is not to flee from your feelings of shame (fleeing will likely increase them), but to ground, focus, and define yourself and turn toward your shame as if it's your friend and partner (which it is). Then you can refocus yourself in respectable and effective ways.

In this fooling-around situation, your *shmanxiety* focused on your present-day behavior, which is easy to understand and change when you take your shame seriously and make amends.

As I write this book, for instance, my *shmanxiety* keeps a close eye on me so that I can stay focused and dedicated over a long period of time. I experienced a lack of motivation a few weeks ago about a chapter that I was avoiding. I edited everything but that chapter, I wrote other chapters, I did other research, but I kept avoiding that chapter. My *shmanxiety* noticed, of course, but I avoided that, too. After a week or so, my *shmanxiety* became more insistent and even annoying, and I started avoiding the entire manuscript because I was so uncomfortable. One morning, I turned to my *shmanxiety* and said out loud, "Look, I know I'm fooling around, but I'm very unsettled about that chapter. There's something in there that I don't want to face, and I'm worried that there's a flaw that will affect the whole book. I'm afraid of letting everyone down." And just like that, my *shmanxiety* settled down, and I was able to get back to writing. Even though I know that emotions will down-regulate or resolve when you work with them empathically, I was surprised by how easy it was to work with my *shmanxiety* when I stopped running from it. We live and learn, don't we, says my *shmanxiety*.

There's a different kind of *shmanxiety* situation that can be a bit more involved or long-lasting, and that's when your anxiety brings an old source of shame back into your conscious awareness.

WHEN YOUR ANXIETY UNEARTHS A PAST SHAME

In chapter 1, I wrote about an internal function of anxiety, which is to examine your resources, memories, mistakes, and failures as they relate to your tasks and projects. Anxiety will perform this inner work in regard to tasks and projects, and it will also perform this work in regard to your other emotions. For instance, your anxiety may focus your attention on old traumas in the case of panic, on broken or weak boundaries in the case of anger, on unworkable situations in the case of depression, or on situations of inequality where you've been taught to see yourself as a second-class citizen (which may bring up many mixed emotions). In regard to shame, anxiety may focus your attention on situations where you let yourself or others down and where it's appropriate to feel ashamed of yourself. Anxiety may also bring your attention to abusive shaming messages because they're getting in the way of your ability to focus and get things done. Anxioneer and DEI professional Anchen Texter from Oregon also focuses on the "should" messages we pick up about how to act, behave, think, look, and so on — because "should" messages nearly always contain externally generated or abusive shame.

In these *shmanxiety* situations — whether your shame is appropriate or whether it's based on abuse — you should ask the shame questions before you engage with your anxiety. When shameful incidents, behaviors, or abusive messages are present in your awareness, it's not time to power through and get your work done; it's time to figure out what's wrong.

If you feel uncomfortable, find ways to soothe yourself, such as the Hands-On Grounding practice, Resourcing, or Rejuvenation. You can also move around or take a walk to regulate yourself, feed yourself something nourishing, or connect with a favorite person or animal who's soothing and comforting. When you're ready, you can return to your *shmanxiety* and see what's going on.

I find that it's helpful to thank my anxiety for bringing this shameful situation to my attention, and then ask the shame question:

SHAME: *Who has been hurt? What must be made right?*

I also find that it's good to write down the answers I receive. If the shame is based on something I did wrong, I can write down what I did and also what I can do now to make it right. If the shame is based on toxic or controlling messages, I can imagine that the paper is a contract and get as much of the message down as I can, and then crumple, tear up, or burn the contract.

Though it's painful to be reminded of times when we hurt others or were hurt ourselves, it's a necessary pain if we want to understand ourselves better, become more accountable and empathic, and evolve as people. It can also be painful to unearth abusive shaming messages that we agreed to for some reason, but this too is a necessary pain if we want to heal from abuse and take charge of the messages and ethics we live by. This pain has a vital purpose, and anxiety is correct to bring this problem to our attention. Thank you, anxiety.

You may need to do some self-reflection and self-healing, speak to a trusted friend, or work with a counselor, but your new awareness can lead you in a more authentic direction. When you feel a sense of completion or distance from this past shame, notice if your anxiety needs any attention. It may not, but if it does, you know the questions to ask.

In the next chapter, we'll explore two emotions that seem to be diametrical opposites: anxiety and depression. One brings you a lot of energy, and the other takes your energy away. This combination of emotions can feel quite puzzling, yet these emotions often arise together for paradigm-changing reasons. We'll approach these emotions empathically and learn to solve the puzzle they present.

9

The Surprising Genius of Depression and Anxiety

Anxiety and depression seem to be completely opposite of each other, yet they often arise together. On one hand, anxiety brings you foresight, focus, and the energy you need to get things done. Depression, on the other hand, can reduce your energy and your sense of urgency, and it may impede you — not only from getting things done, but perhaps from doing anything at all.

If you're a task-focused person who can't finish your tasks, or if you're a procrastinator who can't meet your deadlines, your anxiety may be paired with depression for some reason. This emotional combination may seem perplexing and dysfunctional, but observing these emotions empathically can help you understand what they're doing and how you can work with them (instead of being worked over by them).

Emotion	Gifts and Skills	Internal Questions
SITUATIONAL DEPRESSION arises when things are not working well and you lose the energy to keep going in the ways you previously did. There's always an important reason for situational depression to arise.	The ingenious stop sign of the soul	*Where has my energy gone?* *Why was it sent away?*
ANXIETY (*or WORRY*) is focused on **the future**. It arises to help you look ahead and identify the tasks you need to complete or the deadlines you need to meet.	Foresight, focus, task-completion, procrastination alert!	*What brought this feeling forward?* *What **truly** needs to get done?*

First things first: We're focusing on a form of depression that I call *situational depression*. This is depression that tracks to a situation you can identify, such as an unhappy relationship, an unhealthy work situation, illness, an unsupportive or unequal living environment, and so forth. Because this form of depression relates to a situation you may be able to address and affect, you can work with situational depression on your own (or with a loving friend) in many cases. Situational depression is different from major depression, bipolar depression, seasonal affective disorder, postpartum depression, and other conditions that are best treated by healing professionals.

It's important to separate the *emotion* of depression from conditions that can turn a depressed mood into a troubling state that requires focused care. If your depression is deeper than the situational form I'm focusing on in this chapter, please seek support. If you're not sure about your type of depression, the HelpGuide website (helpguide.org) has excellent information and suggestions for you.

Situational depression is a member of the Sadness Family, and it may help to contrast it with sadness, which arises when it's time to let go of something that isn't working any longer. The Grounding and Focusing practice uses a soft form of sadness to help you let go of things on a regular basis, which helps you remain grounded and emotionally flexible. The difference between sadness and depression is that with sadness, you have a choice about whether you'll let go or not. The empathic practice for sadness is to soften yourself, let go, and then welcome in something that does work, such as relaxation or rejuvenation. With situational depression, however, the choice is no longer yours; something in your life is not only not working, but it's going to cause you trouble (or it's already causing trouble) if you try to keep moving forward. Situational depression will make sure that you cannot move forward until you discover whatever it is that's creating problems in your life.

I call situational depression *ingenious stagnation* because it arises to stop you from moving forward when you should stay still and figure out what's wrong. Situational depression will stop you when you're unaware that you're not feeling well enough, when your behaviors aren't leading you in a healthy direction, when your relationships aren't supportive enough, when your job is wasting your talents, when your living situation or social environment are unhealthy and unequal, and so forth. Situational depression puts on your brakes and reduces your ability to traipse forward doing the wrong thing for the wrong reasons in the wrong place at the wrong time. Situational depression stops you for excellent reasons, but it's vital to learn how to work with it because, as you may know, it can stop you from being able to do anything at all.

If you can slow down, ground and focus yourself, and listen closely, your depression will help you find the unworkable things that need to be addressed. When you can pay attention to your depression in this empathic way, you'll learn about things that need to be dealt with before anything else can happen. After you perform this simple healing action of listening empathically to your depression, then your way forward will be clearer.

If you try to get back to work before you understand and address the problems your situational depression is highlighting, you may experience depression and anxiety (*depresxiety?*) arising together. *Depresxiety* can be a frustrating emotional state that pulls you in seemingly opposite directions. You may want to get things done but stall out and lose your energy. You may try to write lists and organize yourself but end up working on random, meaningless things, or procrastinating in ways that aren't helpful (remember that procrastination can be a helpful behavior for deadline-focused people). Your anxiety may intensify and fill you with a kind of hyperactivation or dread (panic may try to help by bringing you lots of energy, and that might not feel helpful at all), and in response, your depression may intensify as well. Ouch.

Depresxiety can be a deeply uncomfortable state that may lead you to valence both emotions as negative and unwanted, but that would be a mistake. These emotions require skills and understanding, true, but when you know how to work with them, they'll contribute their unique genius and help you identify troubles and prioritize worthwhile tasks that will make a positive difference in the long run.

WORKING WITH ANXIETY AND DEPRESSION TOGETHER

In the third key to emotional genius from chapter 1 (see page 27), I wrote about the importance of understanding mixed or multiple emotions. It's normal for emotions to work in pairs and clusters because each emotion brings you unique skills and intelligence. Depending on your situation, you'll often benefit from the presence of more than one emotion. The unfortunate valencing of emotions as negative or positive reduces our ability to understand or work with them, but our lack of understanding of mixed emotions can really trip us up — especially when emotions as different as anxiety and depression arise together.

When *depresxiety* arises, you'll be in the paradoxical position of experiencing reduced energy and increased energy at the same time. It won't make sense if you look at emotions in a linear way, but if you can understand the interplay between depression and anxiety, their seeming contradictions can lead you to someplace new. In any journey of awareness, healing, or evolution, it's usually the surprising, puzzling, and paradoxical events that initiate meaningful change. When seemingly opposite emotions arise together, they often herald a shift that can't happen in the world of linear, logical, everyday ideas. Paradoxical emotions bring you gifts from the realm of mystery and transformation, and your empathic skills can help you access those gifts.

I notice that *depresxiety* performs a kind of balancing act within you. Sometimes, you and your anxiety will be plugging along skillfully, completing your tasks and meeting your deadlines, so much so that you won't realize that you've lost the thread of meaning in all of your busywork. You may also keep yourself busy so that you can ignore emotional difficulties and avoid your inner life. In instances like this, your depression may arise to slow you down because there's no point to what you're doing; you're wasting your energy or hiding from your true issues, and it's time to stop. If you don't realize that this *depresxiety* is trying to help you, you may ramp up your anxiety to silence your depression, and in so doing, you'll likely initiate a feedback loop in both emotions (not to mention push yourself forward on a path you shouldn't be traveling).

In other situations, you may experience a depressed mood for many reasons, and your anxiety may arise to give you a burst of energy. If you don't understand that your anxiety is trying to help you work *with* your depression, you may mistakenly use your new energy to skate over your depression and prop up the situations that your depression was objecting to in the first place. If you don't cultivate your empathic awareness and your ability to befriend and communicate with your emotions, you and they can spin out and create unnecessary complications. Anxioneer and DEI professional Sandi Davis from California finds that simply getting up and walking outside for a little while can help *depresxiety* take a breath of fresh air, which can relieve some of the discomfort people feel.

The Resourcing practice can also help you work with these paradoxical emotions. Resourcing helps you make room inside yourself for differing or even opposite sensations and ideas, and you can use this practice to gently move back and forth between your depression and your anxiety. When you can create an empathic space where both emotions can coexist inside you, it will be easier to work with and channel them.

The empathic channeling practice for *depresxiety* is simple, but unusual. Though you might think that increasing your energy would be the first step, it's important to focus on your depression first because there's no reason to increase your energy or take action until you understand what's wrong. Luckily, working empathically with your depression does not require energy. All you need to do is to stop, take your depression seriously (instead of pushing forward), and listen to what it has to say. That's it. There's no external action component because depression is about halting all action so that you can take a close look at your situation. This is not a time for chores or bustle, It's a time to stop everything and pay close attention to what's going on in your life. When *depresxiety* is active in you, it's important to focus on the depression questions first because anxiety should not get to work until you find out what the underlying problem is:

SITUATIONAL DEPRESSION: *Where has my energy gone? Why was it sent away?*

Notice that these depression questions don't ask what's wrong with you, what you did wrong, or why you're such a failure. Those kinds of questions belong in the territory of shame (and possibly in the territory of abusive shaming messages that need a serious Burning Contracts session).

Depression's main purpose has very little to do with your self-image or self-esteem, unless those things have caused the problems your depression is trying to address. Does that make sense? Depression shouldn't affect your feelings about yourself unless it is highlighting self-esteem or self-image issues that are causing trouble for you.

Here are two examples that will make this clearer. First, let's imagine that your *depresxiety* arises in response to a miserable job that's just not going to get better. You're a hard worker, and you've applied yourself and kept everything at your rotten job working as well as it can. You have friends there, you've become important to people, and you're proud of your work even though the business is unworthy of you. You probably know the kind of job I'm talking about. When your depression arises in response to this job and you ask the questions about where your energy has gone and why, you may see that all of your good efforts are going into a bottomless pit that can never and will never support you. Once you realize that, you'll be able to make clear-eyed choices about your next steps and refocus your anxiety on tasks that are worth doing or can help you find a better job. This situation is toxic, but you haven't failed.

In a second example, let's imagine that your *depresxiety* arises in response to your inability to find safe or loving friends and partners. No matter how you try to change, you just keep inviting unavailable, disloyal, or abusive people into your life. When you focus on your depression and ask its questions, you may realize that all of your energy is going into refusing to set clear boundaries and refusing to treat yourself with love and respect. In this situation, your poor self-care and your negative self-image are parts of the problem, and you'll need to take a serious look at them if you want anything to get better. Your depression doesn't hate you or want to punish you, but in this situation it needs you to stop and take a long look at how you're creating so much pain for yourself.

In response, your shame may arise because you're doing something wrong (or being something wrong). This is an excellent emotional response because your self-harming behavior needs to change, and shame is the emotion that can help you change it. However, as we've all experienced, feeling this kind of shame can be painful in the best of times, but it can be truly excruciating when we're already feeling depression or *depresxiety*.

If your depression is paired with shame, take a breather here. Inhale gently and exhale out with a sigh, perform the Hands-On Grounding practice, and of course, reach out for support. When shame and depression pair up (*depresshame? shamepression?*), and you have the skills and support you need, you can stop everything, focus on the things you're doing that are hindering or hurting you, and make profound changes with the help of your emotions. However, this can be a difficult process, so it's important to have a supportive friend or counselor by your side.

When you've worked with the problems your depression and shame have alerted you to, your anxiety will have a new set of tasks. In the second example, where your difficulties with self-esteem and self-care are the problem, these new tasks will likely involve therapy or self-healing so that you can learn how to care for yourself and invite only supportive and loving people into your life.

When you discover where your energy has gone and why, you'll be able to turn toward your anxiety and ask its questions:

ANXIETY: *What brought this feeling forward? What **truly** needs to get done?*

You'll probably already know what brought your anxiety forward because you've listened closely to your depression, so your work will likely focus on what *truly* needs to get done. You may not have much energy available to you right away because the situations that depression comes to address are often complex or of long duration. The work of healing may therefore be multifaceted, or it may take a while. But you can use your anxiety's planning skills to create a step-by-step healing strategy and a new focus for whatever energy you do have.

When you're working with *depresxiety*, it's important to live within their paradox instead of trying to pit these two emotions against each other. Many people work with their *depresxiety* in a seesaw fashion: they may use their depression to suppress their anxiety, or they may try to ramp up into anxiety to leap over their depression. Sadly, both tactics treat these emotions disrespectfully. The empathic and respectful practice with *depresxiety* is to befriend both emotions and create a welcoming middle place where your capacity to stop all forward momentum and your ability to plan for and work toward a better future can coexist. When *depresxiety* arises, you have the opportunity to stop and face the difficulties in your life with clear eyes and then refocus your energy and your efforts in new ways so that you can travel in new (and better) directions.

These two emotions need each other. Your anxiety needs the support of your depression so that you won't pour your hard work and excellent planning abilities into something that isn't worth your time or energy. Your depression also needs the support of your anxiety because there are times when you're surrounded by trouble, illness, unhealthy relationships, injustice, inequality, financial distress, instability, or abuse — and it wouldn't be safe to stop everything or drop into your depression. In these situations, your anxiety can help you put your head down and keep going, keep planning, and keep everything running to the best of your ability. Hopefully, when you reach a safer place or find the support you need, your heroic anxiety will be able to step back and let your depression do its important work. It's a delicate and beautiful balancing act with these two, and the key is to remember to include both emotions in any decisions you make — and in anything you do going forward.

In the past few chapters, we've explored the gifts and genius that live in seven allegedly negative emotions (anxiety, fear, confusion, panic, anger, shame, and depression). In the next chapter, we'll look at the many difficulties that can occur when the allegedly positive emotions (happiness, contentment, and joy) are not well-balanced within your emotional realm.

Balancing the Happiness Family and Anxiety

The three emotions in the Happiness Family are marvelous, each in its own way, but all emotions are marvelous in their own ways. As we explore happiness, contentment, and joy, it's important to return to the subject of valencing because valencing causes many problems for these three emotions — and for all of us.

Emotion	Gifts and Skills	Internal Statements
HAPPINESS arises to help you look around you and toward the future with hope and enjoyment.	Amusement, hope, delight, playfulness	*Thank you for this lively celebration!*

Emotion	Gifts and Skills	Internal Statements
CONTENTMENT arises after you've accomplished a task, and it helps you look toward yourself with pride and satisfaction.	Satisfaction, self-esteem, confidence, healthy pride	*Thank you for renewing my faith in myself!*
JOY arises to help you feel a blissful sense of openhearted connection to others, to ideas, or to experiences.	Expansion, inspiration, brilliance, bliss	*Thank you for this wonderful moment!*
ANXIETY (*or WORRY*) is focused on **the future**. It arises to help you look ahead and identify the tasks you need to complete or the deadlines you need to meet.	Foresight, focus, task completion, procrastination alert!	*What brought this feeling forward?* *What **truly** needs to get done?*

Many of the emotions that travel alongside anxiety (such as fear, depression, or shame) are mistakenly valenced as negative. We don't usually learn to love or befriend these emotions, and we don't develop skills beyond clumsy expression or various forms of repression. Instead, we learn to work around these emotions, without them, against them, or despite them.

But valencing emotions positively doesn't fix the problem; in fact, it intensifies the problem and teaches us to treat the allegedly positive emotions in an equally unkind way. Valencing teaches us that the allegedly positive emotions are uniquely healing, preferred, and nearly magical. As a result, we tend to chase after these emotions, hug the life out of them, or try to feel them all of the time — even when we *require* the gifts of other emotions such as anxiety, fear, shame, anger, depression, and so on. Instead of learning to love and befriend our allegedly positive emotions or treat them as normal parts of our emotional realm, we're taught to idealize, entrap, and exploit them.

There's also a troubling issue of percentages here. If you look back at the emotion families in chapter 2, you'll see that three of the four families are misclassified as negative: the Anger Family (anger, apathy, shame, and hatred); the Fear Family (fear, anxiety, confusion, envy, jealousy, and panic); and the Sadness Family (sadness, grief, depression, and the suicidal urge). Only the Happiness Family (happiness, contentment, and joy) is valenced positively. That means that we've been socialized to see just 25 percent of our emotion families as valuable or worthwhile.

But if you count up the individual emotions, you'll see that only three out of the seventeen are allegedly positive, which means that we've been trained to see just 17.6 percent of our emotions as desirable. That's nonsense. Valencing is nonsense! It may help researchers in psychology, psychiatry, or neurology organize emotions so that they can study them, but even in those fields, I see valencing as a huge GIGO problem (garbage in, garbage out). GIGO is a term from computer programming that warns programmers about bad or sloppy code; if the code that runs your program is garbage, your program's output will be garbage too. I've noticed that our GIGO valencing code has programmed us to create a dysfunctional or even abusive relationship with nearly every emotion we have. We're taught to manage, suppress, or shun the allegedly negative emotions and to idolize or overuse the allegedly positive ones. Valencing teaches us to treat all emotions abusively, and that's garbage.

As we interact with our allegedly positive emotions, it's important not to bring garbage programming with us. The hardworking and misunderstood emotions in the Happiness Family deserve better than that. In fact, all of our emotions do.

INTRODUCING THE HAPPINESS FAMILY

Happiness, contentment, and joy are vital emotions that help you look around, at yourself, or toward the future with hope, satisfaction, and delight. Happiness brings you the gifts of amusement, hope, delight, and excitement. Contentment brings you the gifts of satisfaction in a job well done, healthy pride (which is grounded in your efforts and accomplishments), and healthy self-esteem. Joy brings you the gifts of expansiveness, inspiration, and blissful oneness with ideas, living things, nature, and the universe. These three emotions are lovely, but so are all of your other emotions. And just as it is with your other emotions, each of these three has an upside and a downside. You can see this downside very clearly when your happiness, contentment, or joy team up with your anxiety.

As I was writing this book, I was fortunate to be able to speak to Dr. Mary Lamia about the connection between shame and anxiety. At the time, I was dealing with several people who not only blew past deadlines, but didn't let me know that they were going to be late, and I felt that they weren't working very well with their *shmanxiety* (shame and anxiety). We talked about that a bit, and then Mary mentioned something I hadn't thought of. She said that for some people, excitement gets in the way of their ability to get things done because they say yes to too many wonderful things and then can't possibly complete all of them. Aha! I added this chapter to the book and invited the emotions in the Happiness Family to tell me about their relationships with anxiety.

We all know about the upsides to these three emotions because they're written about and spoken about constantly. As I explore their downsides, I notice that problems occur when happiness, contentment, and joy are not well-connected to their fellow emotions. I blame valencing for this because it artificially separates our emotions into two warring camps. That's not how emotions should be treated; it's also not how they work. For instance, the downsides to happiness are that a happy-go-lucky and overly positive attitude can obscure your ability to see problems clearly (the gift of depression), plan intelligently (the gift of anxiety), or say no to things you don't value (the gift of anger). We've all agreed to or bought exciting things when our happiness was left to its own devices and then had to call in more sober emotions to restore our equilibrium.

Happiness is wonderful, and at the same time, it's a member of a large community of emotions that bring you unique gifts and skills. Happiness shouldn't take a leading or solitary position in your emotional life. You'd know this if I were talking about any of the allegedly negative emotions because valencing teaches us to distrust them. But happiness needs its fellow emotions so that it can do its best work.

The downsides to contentment are also related to the quality of its relationship to other emotions, particularly shame. Contentment and shame have a close relationship where your shame keeps a watchful eye on your behavior, and contentment arises when you're behaving in ways that make you feel satisfied with yourself. If your contentment and shame are not well connected, many difficulties may arise. If your shame is overbearing (burn those contracts!), your contentment may not be able to arise because you never do anything well enough to deserve praise (or even a break), according to your abusive shaming messages.

But if your shame is weakened or missing, your contentment may arise for no good reason and congratulate you for every random thing you do. Your contentment is most functional when your shame is functional — when the messages and contracts you agree to are livable, appropriate, and respectful of your individuality and the rights of others. When you and your shame are working well together, your contentment will arise regularly to let you know that you've done a good job and that you're living up to your morals, ethics, and agreements.

The downsides to joy are also connected to its relationship (or lack of relationship) to its fellow emotions. Joy is a peak state — a blissful, limitless, ecstatic state where you drop your boundaries and concerns and become one with someone, something, or everything. It's a marvelous moment in time. But notice that joy lowers your boundaries, which means that your anger and your sense of self will fade away momentarily. Also notice that your concerns disappear, which means that your fear, panic, anxiety, depression, and shame may also fade away. Your sadness, which helps you let go of things that aren't working, may also fade away because joy tends to be an up-regulating state where you open yourself completely to fully embody the joyful experience. Joy is marvelous! However, joy that's allowed to take the lead too often or too long creates problems because it doesn't have the moderating support of its fellow emotions. We have a very apt word for joy that takes the lead and lasts too long: *mania*. Intense and ungrounded joy is the manic and unregulated side of bipolar depression, which can be a brilliant and wildly creative state, but also a quite dangerous one.

It's important to know that peak experiences that rely on joy (such as group prayer, ecstatic dance, fasting, chanting, "love bombing" (showering you with attention, adoration, or gifts), ritualized sex, drug use, and sleep deprivation) are ungrounding and are regularly used by cults and by manipulative individuals to seduce and entrap recruits. We're taught to treat the Happiness Family, and especially joy, as peak emotions that are better than any other emotions; sadly, this makes us perfect victims for anyone who finds a way to harness joy. If anyone or any group tries to recruit your ecstatic joy regularly, be on your guard. Ask your fear, anxiety, panic, anger, and depression to take a very close look at what's going on, talk to trusted friends, research the person or group online, and follow the money! I grew up in a cult and became a cult researcher, and while I learned that there are many mechanisms cults use to recruit and entrap their followers, this exploitation of joy is one of the most powerful.[1] It may seem harmless because people feel so good, but joy that's manipulated to last too long strips away people's grounding, their boundaries, their instincts, and their defenses. There's nothing joyful about that.

I created the Rejuvenation practice to help you (and me!) access joy regularly, not only to give you a lovely healing break, but also to help you know that you don't have to chase after joy. You don't need any substance, person, group, experience, or activity to help you feel joy. Joy lives inside you; it's a normal human emotion that you can access every day. All you need to do is imagine a marvelous place, breathe it in, and rejuvenate yourself with joy. Then you'll naturally move on to your next emotion, your next idea, and your next task. Joy is wonderful, and so are all of your emotions. Each has its place and time, and each has its specific job to do.

The key to working well with your Happiness Family is to know that your emotional skills are just as important when you're happy, contented, and joyful as they are when you're angry, anxious, afraid, sad, or depressed.

WORKING WITH ANXIETY AND
HAPPINESS TOGETHER

Your happiness and your anxiety often work together (*anxappiness?*) because your tasks and projects can be fun, exciting, and delightful. Your happiness can help you feel like anything is possible, or it can create a rush of hope and delight about your work. When *anxappiness* arises during your tasks and projects, it can create a welcome kind of happy dance that helps you keep working. When it does, there's very little for you to do besides enjoy your *anxappiness* and continue with your work.

Emotion	Gifts and Skills	Internal Statements
HAPPINESS arises to help you look around you and toward the future with hope and enjoyment.	Amusement, hope, delight, playfulness	*Thank you for this lively celebration!*
ANXIETY (*or WORRY*) is focused on **the future**. It arises to help you look ahead and identify the tasks you need to complete or the deadlines you need to meet.	Foresight, focus, task completion, procrastination alert!	*What brought this feeling forward?* *What **truly** needs to get done?*

However, if your *anxappiness* arises in the middle of a project to point you in every fun direction *except* toward your tasks, you may need to dig a little deeper. If you're feeling a bit spacey and confused, see chapter 5 to discover what your confusion may be trying to say to you. If you're using happiness to avoid your work, see chapter 8 to find out if your shame is involved or chapter 9 to learn whether your happiness is dancing over the top of your depression. Confusion, shame, and depression contain important gifts, but the endless valencing messages we hear can teach us to run away from them and throw ourselves at happiness. This is not a failing on our part; it's a natural consequence of the GIGO nonsense of valencing. You can challenge and replace valencing with something more respectful by interacting with your emotions empathically and lovingly.

Though you always want to treat your emotions with respect, there's something to be aware of when *anxappiness* arises *before* you agree to a task or a project, and that's an unreasonably positive and overly happy attitude. Dr. Lamia helped me see that overly upbeat people often take on too many tasks and too many projects because everything looks so exciting and hopeful, yippee!

The DEI Anxioneers had a lot to say about why happiness can become unbalanced. Sherry Olander, a DEI professional and instructor from Virginia, noticed a lack of access to anger's gifts; without the moderating influence of anger, happiness might agree to anything, yay! Marion Langford, a DEI professional from Ontario, Canada, noticed that taking on too much feels like a wonderful challenge, but it also helps people avoid rest, downtime, and the gifts of depression. Jeanette Brynn, a DEI professional from Washington State, also noticed that taking on too many exciting projects can help people whose panic plays a huge part in their anxiety. If you always have far too much to do, your *panxiety* can feel necessary, even though it's destabilizing; endlessly exciting busywork might help you overuse your panic instead of finding out why it's so active.

When *anxappiness* is present, your happiness may think that everything is possible, and your anxiety may temporarily agree and get geared up for a sparkling project avalanche. But soon enough, reality will intrude, and your anxiety will need a lot of help, likely from anger, shame, depression, confusion (or panic if you need urgent help with your mountain of too-muchness). Ungrounded happiness can get you and your anxiety into a lot of trouble!

You can avoid this trouble in the future, *before* you agree to any new tasks or projects, by relying on the genius of your boundary-setting anger. You don't have to feel obviously angry to access the gifts of your anger; you just need to mindfully ask the first part of the anger question as you think about taking on new projects:

ANGER: *What do I value?*

Anger can provide an excellent reality check for you and for your *anxappiness*, and it can help you slow down, reset your boundaries, and focus on what's truly important. You can also recruit the genius of your depression because there's an aspect of throwing your energy away in *anxappiness* that may require some self-reflection:

DEPRESSION: *Where has my energy gone? Why was it sent away?*

Depression can help you observe the effects of your behavior clearly, especially when your *anxappiness* is fired up and ready to throw you headlong into too many things. Your depression can help you focus your energy in worthwhile directions. When you're refocused on appropriate and achievable tasks, you can thank your happiness for its lively boost of energy and then ask your anxiety what *truly* needs to get done.

Notice that I'm not asking you to be unkind to your happiness, even when it creates a lot of problems for your anxiety and your other emotions. We're not here to manage or master your emotions; we're here to befriend them and understand them empathically. It's okay if happiness goes on a bender every now and then — just as it's okay for your other emotions to do so. When you have skills and the ability to channel your emotions intentionally, you can use your Empathic Mindfulness practices and request the assistance of your other emotions to bring yourself back to balance. Happiness is lovely, and just like any other emotion, it needs your support (and the support of its fellow emotions) to do its best work. You're a team.

If your happiness is only rarely linked with your anxiety, you may not have the boost of optimism you need to keep working when things get difficult. If your happiness doesn't interact regularly with your anxiety, see the chapters on panic, anger, shame, and depression to see if there's an underlying situation that needs your attention. Your happiness and your anxiety (and the rest of your emotions) will thank you.

WORKING WITH ANXIETY AND CONTENTMENT TOGETHER

When contentment and anxiety work well together (*contentxiety?*), you'll be able to feel proud of yourself for a job well done. Successful task-focused people may experience *contentxiety* dozens of times per day as they wake up on time (yes!), do their household chores (nice!), complete their tasks (good on you!), and face difficult challenges (that was hard, and you did it!). Successful procrastinators, who are focused on deadlines rather than tasks, may feel an underlying hum of contentment (it's all good, my friend) as they subconsciously plan and gather their inner resources on their way toward their deadlines. After the flurry of activity that helps them meet their deadlines, successful procrastinators may feel a large hit of contentment that leans toward joy (*Yes!* This is how you *do* it! *Yeehaw!*).

Contentxiety can help you create a healing back-and-forth relationship between your good work and your healthy self-regard, almost like a perpetual motion machine, where your good work leads you to a sense of healthy pride that leads you to want to do more good work. *Contentxiety* may help you do your work and also *want* to do your work. Good job, *contentxiety*.

Emotion	Gifts and Skills	Internal Statements
CONTENTMENT arises after you've accomplished a task, and it helps you look toward yourself with pride and satisfaction.	Satisfaction, self-esteem, confidence, healthy pride	*Thank you for renewing my faith in myself!*
ANXIETY (*or WORRY*) is focused on **the future**. It arises to help you look ahead and identify the tasks you need to complete or the deadlines you need to meet.	Foresight, focus, task completion, procrastination alert!	*What brought this feeling forward?* *What **truly** needs to get done?*

However, this balanced relationship between good work and appropriate pride requires the input of your other emotions. You need anger's influence to help you set boundaries around what you truly value, or you may take on too many tasks just to feel good about yourself. Anxioneer and DEI professional Marion Langford from Ontario, Canada, notices this tendency in people who take on too many projects so that they can feel like task-completing superheroes. This is not necessarily a problem, but it can be a sign that a person doesn't feel everyday contentment or happiness on a regular basis — or that they're using overwork to avoid other emotions and issues. If your *contentxiety* regularly takes on far too much, you'll need the moderating influence of your depression to help you understand where your energy is going and why.

Shame is also a necessary counterbalance to *contentxiety* because without it, you may hold an unbalanced view of your talents and abilities. Contentment should arise after you've done good work, and good work is something your shame is intimately involved with: Do you have the skills you need? Are you living up to your agreements? Are you getting things done properly and on time? Are you honest with yourself about your abilities? Are you treating others with respect? Just being able to take on and complete a mountain of projects doesn't mean that you're good at them. In fact, overburdening yourself will likely mean that you can only give a portion of yourself to each project and perhaps do sloppy work. If your shame is awake and functional, it will gently question what you're doing and help you burn your contracts and make better choices in the future.

But if your shame isn't available to you, your *contentxiety* may fill your life with too much activity and not enough serious contemplation. You may also fool yourself into thinking you're a bigger deal than you are. I experienced this with a business consultant I hired. She talked a big game and made a lot of promises that didn't ever pan out because she was in way over her head and too busy to take stock of herself. When I questioned her about the ways she had not fulfilled her contract, she didn't have any idea about how to respond. In her silence, I could sense a kind of empty space where her shame should have been. All that she could say was that she was sorry I felt that way. I told her that wasn't an apology, and again there was silence followed by a list of how talented she was and how other people thought she was awesome. We eventually got things worked out to a certain extent, but I sense that it was only because she needed to feel *contentxiety* again, and not because she had found a way to feel her appropriate shame.

Contentment helps you feel proud of yourself for a job well done, and it can create a delightful emotional partnership with your anxiety, but be aware. Your *contentxiety* works best when it's well-connected to its friends, anger, shame, and depression. In fact, each of your emotions can only do their best work when they're connected to the healing influences of your entire emotional community.

If you rarely feel contented about yourself or your work, see the chapters on shame, depression, and anger; there may be contracts to burn and boundaries to set before your contentment and your *contentxiety* can arise.

WORKING WITH ANXIETY AND JOY TOGETHER

When anxiety and joy work together (*joyxiety?*), you can feel a sense of transcendence in your work. Many artists talk about feeling elated as they create and being so inspired by their artistic process that the everyday world, time, and even their bodily needs fade away.

Emotion	Gifts and Skills	Internal Statements
JOY arises to help you feel a blissful sense of openhearted connection to others, to ideas, or to experiences.	Expansion, inspiration, brilliance, bliss	*Thank you for this wonderful moment!*
ANXIETY (*or WORRY*) is focused on **the future**. It arises to help you look ahead and identify the tasks you need to complete or the deadlines you need to meet.	Foresight, focus, task completion, procrastination alert!	*What brought this feeling forward?* *What **truly** needs to get done?*

Though I've learned to manage it, I can be so joyously transported by writing that I forget to eat, drink water, or even look up from the computer for hours at a stretch. This is a marvelous experience of inspiration and flow, but it's not sustainable over a long career, and my body does not appreciate hours of unintentional fasting and immobility. My other emotions have thankfully stepped in: my anger has taught me to set boundaries around my writing schedule; my depression has taught me to manage my writing energy more sensibly; my shame has taught me to take better care of my body; and my anxiety has helped me learn how to complete other tasks and pay attention to the people in my life during intense writing periods.

Joyxiety is lovely, but like joy itself, it's a peak state that you're not meant to live in every day. I've learned this from watching my artist friends who deal with bipolar manias. One of my friends will shift into a manic *joyxiety* state and paint dozens of intricate, full-sheet watercolors in a few weeks. They're breathtakingly beautiful and complex (you've never seen watercolors like these), but she doesn't eat or sleep regularly during these periods of intense inspiration. When she was younger, she could get away with this behavior, but as she matured, married, and had children, her manic *joyxiety* periods required the support of many people so that her life wouldn't fall apart and her children would be cared for.

My late mother was an artist, and she and I became part of this painter friend's support structure when she was in her mid-fifties and all but one of her children had become estranged from her. Mom and I did what we could to create boundaries and structure around her creative periods (she was on medications, but only intermittently because they had debilitating side effects), and we tried to help her ground her endlessly overexcited ideas about money-making opportunities. But we failed because the intensity of her *joyxiety* overwhelmed everything — her family and friends, her other emotions, and eventually her health and sanity. I realize that I'm writing about a person with an unmanaged psychological condition, but being with her helped me understand the consequences of limitless ecstatic *joyxiety*. I also saw the consequences of limitless joy in the cult I was in and the cults I studied. Joy is a powerful, all-consuming peak state, and the power of all-consuming joy carries danger with it.

You would know about that danger if we were focusing on a powerful negatively valenced emotion here (such as rage, grief, or the suicidal urge); you would see the danger clearly. But our vision and intelligence about the emotions in the Happiness Family are obscured by valencing. We've been taught to see the emotions in the Happiness Family as perfectly positive and always necessary, and as such, we've been taught to be deeply ignorant about them. Joy, like every other emotion, has an upside and a downside. And joy, like every other emotion, needs loving and empathic support from you and from its fellow emotions.

Your *joyxiety* can be a blissful state that brings inspiration and transcendence to your work; it's brilliant. And at the same time, it requires awareness, grounding, boundaries, reality checks, down-regulation, self-care, and all of your Empathic Mindfulness practices so that you can maintain your balance in the presence of its peak experiences. Or as the title of Buddhist teacher Jack Kornfield's famous book tells us, "after the ecstasy, the laundry."[2]

If you rarely feel joy, remember that the Rejuvenation practice recruits your joy intentionally and gently so that you can feel it without being carried away. Also, see the chapters on shame, panic, and depression; there may be old contracts, old traumas, or a situation of imbalance that needs to be addressed before your joy can arise freely. And of course, a visit to your health-care team or a counselor may be supportive when your joy is silenced for some reason.

We've looked at nine emotions that can work directly with your anxiety to either help you do your work or impede you for important reasons. Of course, your anxiety may also work with emotions that we haven't focused on here. If so, I hope that these chapters have given you ideas about how to work empathically and lovingly with your mixed emotions. Remember that channeling your emotions can be as simple as increasing your vocabulary (so that you can identify your emotions at many levels of activation) and then asking their specific questions. Your emotions want to communicate with you, and they want to help you; that's their job. Whether they arise singly or in pairs or groups, your emotions always bring you the support you need to think, decide, act, love, dream, heal, and do your best work.

In the final two chapters, we'll look at how to live well when your anxiety is required on a regular basis — either in your work, or in response to challenging situations and troubling times.

PART III

Supporting Your
ANXIETY
in the World

11

When Anxiety Is a Vital
Tool in Your Career
(and Your Life)

I consult in businesses and organizations to help people create work environments where emotional awareness and healthy empathy can flourish. People hire me to address unique situations and problems, but the solutions always come down to this: everyone in the workplace needs emotional skills and shared communication practices to help them deal with difficulties, understand each other in the context of their work, and interact skillfully with their colleagues, customers, and members of the public. These solutions are always tailored to each organization's unique needs, but the bottom line is that professionals need to develop shared emotional and empathic skills in order to do their best work as a team.

A few years ago, I began to notice what I call *hidden emotion professionals*, or people whose work demands that they stay in one (or more) emotion in order to get their work done. For instance, hospice workers could be seen as *grief professionals* who help people as they die and support bereaved families before and after their loved one's death. People who set boundaries and focus on rules and precise behaviors, such as police officers, judges, and accountants, could be seen as *anger professionals*. People who help others let go of stress and things they don't need anymore, such as massage therapists or professional home declutterers, could be seen as *sadness professionals*. And people whose work requires that they focus and plan far into the future (such as stock traders, film producers, or construction developers) could be seen as *anxiety professionals*.

I first saw this clearly when I consulted in a construction development firm in a large metropolitan city. I spent two days per month with a team of a dozen people who developed large skyscrapers and multibuilding projects involving hundreds of millions of dollars and many moving parts.

As I got to know this high-achieving group, I saw them as brilliant and talented hard workers who loved to laugh between periods of intense focus on multiple projects, yet something confused me about them. I spent time with them after work, and I noticed that they drank a lot. I don't drink at all, so I see drinking as unusual, but these people drank *a lot*. From their conversations, I learned that heavy drinking was normal for them at the end of their workweek, at office parties, and at the end of big projects. This didn't compute for me because these were well-paid, well-treated, environmentally conscious, health conscious, and politically active people with excellent social support. The heavy drinking didn't make sense.

One morning, after a night out with the group where drinking was their main activity, I asked some casual questions about their workflow and how their projects played out from beginning to end. I had been focusing so much attention on their relationships and their work environment that I wasn't clear about what their work actually entailed. When they explained just one of their current projects from beginning to end, I had a big aha moment: these people were *anxiety professionals*!

The team explained that their work lived far in the future — sometimes five to eight years in the future. They would purchase existing high-rises or whole blocks of buildings, wait until all of the individual leases ran out (or they would buy them out), demolish the buildings, build entirely new ones, and then re-lease the suites, entire floors, or whole buildings to new companies. Their projects were enormously complex and multifaceted, and nearly all of the facets were based on speculation and optimistic hope about the future (these people needed to be *anxappiness* professionals too, always believing that their professional future would be wonderful).

There was some grounding, of course, because their city was vibrant and had been popular throughout its history. Their firm was well-respected, and many successful companies wanted to move into their shiny new buildings. But even so, the team's present-day lives consisted of speculation and hope that everything would go well: that building regulations would work out in their favor, that multiple subcontractors would perform well, that the real estate market would continue to grow, that interest rates would remain stable, that local government would remain supportive, and that a crowd of suitable new lessees would appear in the coming years (among many other things). Each person on the team required expertise and intelligence, excellent interpersonal skills, and wide-ranging awareness of all of the moving pieces, but what they required most of all was continually activated anxiety about tasks and projects that existed in the far-away future.

These anxiety professionals' tasks and deadlines were continual, so they could complete things and feel the relief of completion regularly, and yet there were aspects of their projects that were so far in the future that their anxiety needed to be on alert most of the time. Team members told me that they thought about their work constantly and checked off details in their heads at night and on weekends, or they woke up in the early morning with new ideas about things that needed attention. Their team regularly exceeded the goals that were set for them, yet the anxiety that was necessary for their future-based work wouldn't let them rest, even on vacations. After they explained their work, I realized that their seemingly incongruous heavy drinking may have been the only way they had found to relax their bodies and quiet their overactive minds.

With their input, I created a list of supportive practices to help them address their work-related anxiety (see "Supportive Practices for Anxiety Professionals" on page 190) so that it wouldn't burn them out. The most supportive thing, however, was that they could now identify themselves as anxiety professionals and reframe their approach to their constant activation, and to each other. They learned to check in with each other carefully instead of unintentionally disturbing each other or increasing each other's anxiety about tasks and deadlines. Though their work remained intense, highly detailed, and fast-paced, they now had many options besides heavy drinking to help their overworked systems settle down.

WHEN YOUR ANXIETY IS A VITAL TOOL AT HOME, TOO

There are many situations at home that require your anxiety to be on task: paying bills; maintaining your home; dealing with clutter; moving or looking for housing; building or fixing your home; caring for children, pets, or adults; managing the current, future, and possible outcomes of health issues; and so forth. People working outside the home are not the only anxiety professionals.

As you read the following practices, feel free to apply them to your home environment. When you can plan for and solve for situations of increased anxiety, you'll create a healthy home for your emotions, and at the same time, you'll lighten the load of everyone in your home.

You may have noticed that when parents or family members don't work well with their emotions, someone in the family may take on those emotions and begin to act them out. When I was a little girl, I acted out the anger for my anger-avoiding parents, and it took me many years to shake off that behavior and learn how to work with my own anger appropriately. If someone in your family (or your workplace) is acting out a great deal of anxiety, certainly help them find support, but also note how the people in their environment are dealing with anxiety. If others are avoiding, repressing, or working clumsily with their anxiety — if they're creating an emotionally unregulated environment — they're creating an unhealthy situation for the person acting out the anxiety, but they're also creating an unhealthy situation for themselves. Everyone needs support in situations like this. The following practices should help.

SUPPORTIVE PRACTICES FOR ANXIETY PROFESSIONALS

Anxiety professionals spend much of their workday (or home life) in a forward-focused and activated state, so they need a soothing, reliable, grounding, and calming atmosphere to balance them. These following suggestions can help anxiety professionals balance the necessary activation their careers demand with the regular grounding and down-regulation their bodies require. This is not an exhaustive list, and you may have already found excellent ways to support yourself when your work or home life requires continually activated anxiety. Of course, use only what makes sense to you, and substitute your own practices if they work better.

WORKDAY PRACTICES

- Listening to your emotions
- Paying attention to any emotions that arise alongside your anxiety; they may be offering support (see part II, "When Anxiety Teams Up with Other Emotions")
- Paying attention to the emotions of others
- Developing shared emotional skills and communication practices with your colleagues
- Making lists and crossing off the tasks you've completed, or envisioning your projects and creating mini-deadlines along the way
- Remaking your lists and reorganizing them

- Creating order and managing small problems in a regular rhythm
- Sighing and exhaling downward to ground yourself and let go of tension
- Grounding several times throughout the day
- Practicing Conscious Complaining
- Practicing Rejuvenation
- Reducing caffeine, or stopping intake by 2:00 pm so that you can clear the caffeine before bedtime
- Finding social support
- Asking for help
- Being listened to
- Being with supportive colleagues
- Laughing out loud and being silly

HOME PRACTICES

- Lazing around with no purpose
- Being with supportive friends and family
- Being in nature
- Listening to your emotions
- Paying attention to any emotions that arise alongside your anxiety; they may be offering support (see part II, "When Anxiety Teams Up with Other Emotions")
- Using your Empathic Mindfulness practices regularly
- Laughing out loud and being silly
- Playing with animals

- Finding social support
- Asking for help
- Being listened to
- Doing art or engaging with music, drama, dance, or design
- Crying when you need to
- Meditating (be aware that some forms of meditation and deep breathing may worsen your anxiety; if they do, move on to another form right away)
- Getting heated up (sweating is important)
  - Sweat-producing exercise
  - Awesome sex or masturbation
  - Sauna, hot tub, or hot bath until you're utterly relaxed
- Drinking alcohol, if it doesn't interfere with your sleep or impair you the next day
- Using marijuana, if it doesn't interfere with your sleep or impair you the next day
- Taking antianxiety medications or beta-blockers, if you need them
- Curating good, healthy sleep[1]

HOW MANAGERS AND BUSINESS OWNERS CAN SUPPORT EMOTION PROFESSIONALS

If you understand the kinds of emotional labor you require from your workers and colleagues, you can create an environment that supports them and solves for the specific emotional workloads they carry. Here are some simple examples:

- **Anxiety** professionals (think future-based planners) need *fewer* changes or surprises in the workplace (they're already dealing with too much change and input); reliability and stability; grounding; physical comfort; quiet and privacy; and loving humor. Think about what would feel supportive for you if you were under constant demand, pressed for time, and dealing with endless tasks and projects that play out in a future you can't control.

- **Anger** professionals (think police, lawyers, or accountants) need: workplace changes that they have choices about (so that they can choose what they value); fluid and flexible structure (to balance the often-rigid aspects of their work lives); many opportunities to relax and reduce their focus; and loving or absurd humor (not sarcasm, which is a form of anger and can overload these professionals). Imagine what would support you if your entire workday was focused on creating (or enforcing) structure, rules, and boundaries that you must uphold and apply but may have no control over.

- **Grief** professionals (think hospice nurses and funeral directors) need: reliable daily structure (because grief is so fluid); boundaries between clients; private space in the workplace; clear and self-directed thresholds between their work time and break time (to give them the opportunity to create and maintain boundaries); and opportunities to express and share morbid humor and sarcasm (sarcasm is a form of anger, and it sets boundaries). Think about what would support you if your work was about helping people live with the very real specter of death, providing comfort in difficult situations, providing empathy at all times, and helping families mourn their losses.

Of course, your workplace is unique, and the emotional labor that occurs there is unique too. These suggestions are meant to help you start thinking about the emotional demands you and your colleagues face. Also, note that people in different positions within your workplace will have different emotional demands, such that a person in tech support may deal with entirely different kinds of emotional situations than a person in research and development does.

As you explore the emotional environment of your workplace, pay attention to the ways people cope, whether other emotions are stepping in to help, or whether behaviors like heavy drinking are being used for support. How are your people managing the emotional demands of your workplace, and what can you do to support your people and solve for the emotional demands your workplace creates?

Creating an emotionally well-regulated workplace is, of course, out of the scope of this book on anxiety, but I want you to know that whether you're an employee, a manager, or a business owner, there are many things you can do to increase the health and well-being of everyone in your workplace. Creating an empathic and caring environment will support your anxiety (and the anxiety of everyone in your workplace) because when your emotional environment is well regulated, your anxiety won't have to be constantly on guard just to keep your work life functional. Empathy and emotional awareness can help you create working environments that are conducive to work and to the health and well-being of everyone in the workplace.

And of course, creating an empathic and caring environment in your home is just as important as creating one at work. When you have an emotionally well-regulated environment in your home, your anxiety and the rest of your emotions will have the time and space they need to do their best work — and so will everyone who's lucky enough to live with you.

In the final chapter, we'll explore ways to support yourself in troubling situations and troubling times when your anxiety and your panic may need to be on high alert. These two emotions — alone or together — can keep you safe in unsafe situations, yet they need your support, your empathy, and your love to do their best work.

12

Self-Care in
Anxious Times

I'm writing this book from my home in Sonoma County, California, which was devastated by wildfires last year and inundated by floods this year. In the news each week, I learn about a new scandal, a new mass shooting, a new situation of national or international chaos, multiple refugee crises, and seemingly endless instances of injustice, prejudice, racism, violence, inequality, ecological volatility, and devastating political and judicial incompetence. On some days, there's so much terrible news that I have to take my rage, grief, panic, and depression out for a Conscious Complaining (yelling) walk so that we can all blow off some steam, feel into the horror of the world, and find our center once again. And all the while, my anxiety waits, watching.

When the world is off-balance and the future is uncertain or alarming, each of your emotions will notice and respond in their own ways, but your anxiety is perhaps more impacted by this kind of instability than your other emotions are. In times of social and political upheaval, the troubles around you may be so complex that your anxiety could be active twenty-four hours a day and never attain a sense of having learned enough, thought enough, planned enough, or done enough to prepare for the future.

When you're surrounded by uncertainty and your anxiety is on task constantly, it's also natural for your panic to arise to see what can be done. But as you know, *panxiety* can feel intense and destabilizing. In difficult and *panxiety*-provoking times, trouble brews outside of you, and if you don't have *panxiety*-specific skills or practices, trouble brews inside of you as well. It can sometimes feel as if there's no safe place to be.

Anxioneers and DEI professionals Anchen Texter from Oregon and Amanda Ball from Massachusetts are in their thirties, and they've noticed that people their age deal with a lot of anxiety and *panxiety* about their uncertain futures. Anchen noticed that families are keeping their young people closer to them for longer than they did in earlier generations and that many people in her generation are unsure about their place as adults. She laughed about the concept of "adulting" and talked about all of the courses she's seen on how to "adult." Anchen wondered if the loss of clear transitions into adulthood means that anxiety is constantly on edge, always waiting for the next phase of life to begin.

Amanda suggested that staying in an extended childhood and refusing to make the transition into full adulthood might be an anxiety and *panxiety* response to a future that doesn't look manageable or hopeful, so why bother? Amanda pointed to climate change, the breakdown of our political systems, famines, wars, inequality, injustice, America's gun crisis, racism, homophobia, sexism, and the student loan crisis. *Panxiety* could go on and on about all the trouble. Considering this, it's understandable that depression and apathy may be helping many young people deal with their sense of overwhelm. Of course, not all people in their thirties feel this way, but it's an interesting observation from people within that generation.

I've also been interested to watch the generation of teens today who are stepping forward to deal with problems that adults have failed to address. Swedish teenager Greta Thunberg responded to her *panxiety* about our future by starting a solitary school strike for the climate in front of the Swedish parliament building in 2018. Greta's strike quickly gathered a large international community of supporters and fellow school strikers, and she was nominated for the Nobel peace prize in 2019. I love Greta's approach because she names the intense emotions she feels with precision and demands that we all take the troubles of the world seriously; she's a *panxiety* shrine and a *panxiety* professional. The sad fact that many adults tried to bully and stop Greta speaks not only to their inability to work with (or even face) their own *panxiety*, but also to a serious shame impairment that weaponizes their lack of emotion-regulation skills.

Greta has said that she got the idea for her strike from watching the Parkland students from Florida who rose up as voices for gun control after they watched their classmates die senselessly in one of the endless mass shootings that we let happen regularly in the United States. To my eye, these young people are choosing healing actions in response to their intense *punxiety* and setting clear boundaries around what they value with their *angerxiety*. These young people are responding to the catastrophic failures of adults by channeling their emotions appropriately, and I admire their energy and their vision.

But I also see people who are choosing destructive actions and setting violent boundaries in response to their *panxiety* and *angerxiety* about the troubles of the world. There's a worldwide increase in extremism, prejudice, nationalism, populism, fundamentalism, end-times beliefs, and hate groups, and to my eye, what we're seeing are the natural consequence of our tragically poor emotional education and our related lack of robust empathic skills. These problems with emotions and empathy aren't the fault of the individuals who are caught up in these destructive movements (our emotional training is universally terrible), but they're the fuel that keeps them there.

For many people, intense emotions like *panxiety* and *angerxiety* are excruciating and unlivable, and anything that provides rigid certainty, blames others (including Greta Thunberg) for all the problems, and promises to get rid of the problems will be dangerously seductive — and dangerously destructive to us all. People so often downplay emotional skills or belittle them as soft skills, but those people are not paying attention. Emotional and empathic skills are at the center of everything you think, everything you do, and everything you are. When you know how to work with your emotions, you can weather any kind of trouble and bring your empathy to even the most difficult situations. When you have emotional skills and empathic skills, you can heal your life and become able to heal the problems of our world.

Anxioneer and DEI professional Marion Langford from Ontario, Canada, says that when you're feeling overwhelmed by the troubles of the world (or when new troubles or responsibilities get added to your life), you need to double your self-care, but what we notice is that many people instead reduce their self-care by half or more. If you look at the Healing Actions/Dubious Actions chart in chapter 6 (see page 127), you'll see that many people gravitate toward the dubious actions when trouble is brewing. That's understandable, but in the long run, it's not helpful or sustainable for anyone. It's also not helpful for the world because if we're all distracted, dissociated, ungrounded, isolated, and incapacitated, there will be no one left to address our collective troubles and devise workable solutions.

Each chapter in this book has offered ideas and practices to help you develop the emotional awareness, Empathic Mindfulness, and self-care skills you need to live consciously and intentionally with your anxiety and its fellow emotions. Chapter 11 gives you lists of practices you can use when your anxiety needs to be highly activated on a regular basis, and chapter 6 explores what you need when your *panxiety* is activated over long periods of time. Regular exercise, rest and relaxation, mindfulness breaks, healthy self-talk, good food, loving relationships, supportive community, quiet time, restorative sleep, bodywork, playtime, and laughter are necessary if your emotions are on high alert. Each of the Empathic Mindfulness practices I've shared will also help you work skillfully with your emotions.

All these things can help you weather anxiety-provoking times so that your emotional life, your body, your relationships, and your outlook will remain healthy and grounded — but there's also a group of supportive concepts that can help you thrive in difficult situations and difficult times.

THE FOUR PILLARS OF A WHOLE LIFE

In 2002, my husband, Tino Plank, attended a retreat with mythologist Michael Meade, African elder and shaman Malidoma Somé, poet and activist Luis Rodriguez, and Buddhist teacher Jack Kornfield. These men gathered together to share their ideas for how to live a whole life in a fractured world. Their retreat revolved around what they called the four pillars of a whole life: art, practice, ritual, and community. These concepts helped Tino ground and deepen his own understanding of how to live, and they're something we've relied on ever since. I also teach these concepts in DEI Self-Care courses and retreats, and I explain them this way:

Art is the image-rich way you express your truth in the outer world.

Practice is the image-rich way you express your truth in the inner world.

Ritual is the process of reaching out to nature, your emotions, and the sacred for support, healing, and mentoring.

Community is the process of reaching out to others for mutual support, communion, learning, teaching, laughing, loving, caring for each other, and tending the heart of the world.

In this book, I've focused on practice and ritual. Your Empathic Mindfulness practices help you tend to your inner world with empathy and skill, and many of these practices are also healing rituals. Conscious Complaining, Burning Contracts, Rejuvenation, and Conscious Questioning for Anxiety are rituals that help you request healing support and mentoring from your emotions themselves. In DEI, we teach many other rituals for emotions like grief, shame, depression, and hatred, and we find that bringing a ritual aspect to your emotional life has deeply healing effects.

Art and community, however, are equally important pillars, and it can take work to integrate them into your daily life. It's very sad that art has been moved out of our schools, professionalized, criticized, and commercialized, because art is simply your unique way of expressing your experiences. Your art can consist of movements, words, imagery, sounds, colors, ideas, concepts, structures, activities, or performances, and the lovely thing about your personal artistic expression is that it doesn't have to be any good, and it doesn't have to make sense to anyone else. What I notice empathically about art is that it helps people express themselves emotionally, often in ways they never could through talking or thinking about their emotions. Art can access the wordless part of us that sees the world in unusual ways and carries unusually deep knowledge. Artistic expression can also help us bring hazy ideas (hello, confusion) into clearer focus so that we can understand previously mystifying concepts. Art can bring you surprising new ideas, and it can give you the freedom to express yourself and know yourself in deep and healing ways.

Developing your art is a lifelong process, and it's also a lifelong practice of making the time and space for your art to flourish. If you're in a difficult situation that engages your *panxiety*, your *angerxiety*, or your *depresxiety*, you may find that doing your art can help you bring clarity to all of your emotions. You can also lean into the fourth pillar of a whole life by joining a community of artists, singers, dancers, musicians, weavers, poets, and so on, so that you'll have support for your artistic nature and also provide support to others.

Community is the fourth pillar of a whole life, and it's a vital part of maintaining your balance when your life is difficult and the world is filled with trouble and uncertainty. Community is especially important when you're dealing with ongoing situations of social inequality, illness, poverty, or a lack of safety. In these unequal or unhealthy situations, your social insight may need to be pitched at a higher frequency, so it's important to surround yourself with people who know what you're going through, value your social insights, and respect you as an individual.

The emotional labor you perform in unequal or unhealthy environments can be tiring, so it's good to develop nourishing relationships and welcoming spaces where your social insight and your anxiety (or *panxiety*) can rest and relax. I've noticed that what marginalized people call "safe spaces" are spaces where they don't have to perform emotional labor or be vigilant about offending people in the dominant culture. In safe spaces, people can just be people, and their anxiety can stand down.

Community is also vital when you're facing larger social ills: injustice, inequality, prejudice, violence, and degradation. Something I've found healing is to support existing communities or organizations that have been working for many decades on the problems that concern me. I have a lot of concerns, so I belong to a lot of organizations and communities, but I curate them (thank you, anger) because I don't want to be overwhelmed by blatant emotional appeals or the often-unskilled emotional behaviors of people who are fervent about justice and equality. I focus instead on the work that's being done, the infrastructure that's being built, and the influence that these organizations are wielding in the service of healing and justice. These communities help me and my emotions function effectively even when the world is on fire (literally, in the case of my home county last year).

Another place that I've found healing community is online. I know that many people think an online life is isolating and antisocial, but as a writer, I live a great deal of life in my mind, and the Internet has helped me connect to brilliant minds and souls all over the world. I've developed an online learning site called Empathy Academy where we create and nurture empathic community across the world every day, and I run and belong to many supportive groups on Facebook, where I can meet people I'd never know if I stayed in the so-called real world of my hometown. A special aspect to my online life is that I have met and befriended many disabled people whose mobility or language issues prevent them from engaging easily in person, and my world has been enriched because of them.

These four pillars have formed the foundation of my and Tino's life for over sixteen years, and they've also been a part of the lives of DEI students and professionals all over the world. But I have to tell you that we all regularly fail to keep every pillar standing straight; it's a work in progress at all times. But it's necessary work if we want to live whole lives that we, our anxiety, and our entire emotional realm can be proud of. I send many thanks to Michael, Malidoma, Luis, and Jack for bringing this model of the four pillars into the world.

EMBRACING YOUR WHOLE EMOTIONAL LIFE

Anxiety does so much to keep our lives working, and I'm so glad that we've been able to spend extended time listening to it, watching it, discovering its genius, and learning its language. We've learned so much about how anxiety works with its fellow emotions and how much our emotions rely on each other to help us complete our tasks and projects successfully.

In chapter 4, I shared our DEI motto for anxiety: "There's always enough time for every important thing." But I see something in it now that I didn't see when I started writing this book. The key word in this motto is *important*, which means that your anger is on the job, identifying what you value and setting boundaries around things that are unimportant. But depression is also working to verify that you're not throwing away your energy. And shame is on task to make sure that you're making enough time for what's important and living up to your agreements. In fact, all of your emotions are present, watching over you, supporting you, and helping your anxiety get your important work done.

I wrote this book about anxiety, but what I discovered is that anxiety cannot act alone. It needs support from you and your Empathic Mindfulness practices; it needs the support of its fellow emotions; it needs anxiety-specific practices; and it needs the whole-life support of art, practice, ritual, and community. In fact, all of your emotions do.

I think it's funny, but perfect, that I entered the world of anxiety with an organized, step-by-step plan to understand it and ended up understanding more about emotions, self-care, and human nature as a whole. Thank you, my friend anxiety, for tricking this task-focused person into completing a massive project (in the final moments of a deadline) that I could never have envisioned on my own. I hope this book makes up for my earlier ignorance about you and lets you know how important you are to me, and to our waiting world.

I thank you, too, for reading this book and taking this journey into the emotional realm with me. I hope that you, your anxiety, and all of your emotions have new ideas, skills, and practices to help you live well and nurture the unique genius that lives inside you. Take care of yourself; we need your voice, your heart, and your presence in our community.

Acknowledgments

I always thank my husband, Tino Plank, first because his love and support made the world safe enough for my writing (and my heart) to flourish. He is my sounding board, my first reader, my argument partner, a magnificent anxiety shrine, and my deepest friend. My time with Tino has been a delight and a gift, and this book could not exist without him. I thank him today and every day.

I thank my friend and editor Haven Iverson and the acquisitions team at Sounds True for asking for a book on a single emotion, and for choosing anxiety first; it's such a good idea! Haven is a careful, responsive, and hilarious reader, and her edits always make my books deeper and more valuable. Many thanks also go to Dr. Mary Lamia for recognizing the value of anxiety from within the heavily valenced field of psychology; that's a marvelous form of emotional genius and compassion.

Amanda Ball is a brilliant and feisty young woman who focused the coursework and internship for her master's degree in counseling on the work in my book *The Language of Emotions* (which had never been done). She came to a weeklong retreat I taught at the Kripalu Center for Yoga and Health, and at lunch on the final day, she told me of her plans. She kindly informed me that she'd do this work with me or without me. I chose *with*, and a marvelous partnership began. Amanda is the reason Dynamic Emotional

Integration exists, and I thank her every day. I also thank DEI professionals Sherry Olander and Jen Nate for taking lead roles alongside Amanda as DEI instructors at Empathy Academy so that I could write this book. Thank you, my friends.

I also thank my friends and DEI colleagues, the wonderful Anxioneers, who gathered together on Zoom videoconferencing to talk, laugh, feel, argue, and get to know our friend anxiety. These licensed DEI professionals are (in alphabetical order) Sarah Alexander from Oregon; Jennifer Asdorian from Washington, DC; Zakyeya Atcha from Lancashire, UK; Pia Ault from Dubai, UAE; Amanda Ball from Massachusetts; Francine Bélanger from Ontario, Canada; Jeanette Brynn from Washington State; Sandi Davis from California; Juliet Holding from London, UK; Camilla Jørgensen from Copenhagen, Denmark; Marion Langford from Ontario, Canada; Jessica Moore from Arizona; Jennifer Nate from Alberta, Canada; Sherry Olander from Virginia; Michael Perez from Florida; Tino Plank from California; Anchen Texter from Oregon; and Andrea Watkins from Colorado.

And of course, I thank my good friend anxiety for helping me throughout the years, forgiving me for overlooking it, and mentoring me as I wrote this book. Thank you, anxiety, for talking with me, walking with me, waking me up early, introducing me to your emotion pals, bothering me when I was off task and off topic, making me laugh, and sharing your gifts and your genius.

I also thank *you* for reading this book. Thank you for embracing anxiety, thank you for spending time with these ideas, and thank you for bringing more emotional awareness and empathy to our waiting world. Be well.

Appendix:
Helping Children
Embrace Their Anxiety

Children need support as they learn to feel and work with their emotions, but luckily, because they're relatively new to language (and to our mostly damaging, valenced training about emotions), they're easier to work with than adults. Helping children learn about emotions is a matter of communication, play, and good timing.

I developed a series of imaginary games to help children learn to identify and play with their emotions when they feel calm and interested. As you may already know, trying to teach children about emotions and emotion regulation when they're feeling intense or destabilized is not workable; emotional skills form a foundation that children can rely on when they're feeling intense emotions, but they must build that foundation first.

Depending on their age, you can help younger, early-speaking, or nonspeaking children identify emotions by simply naming their emotions for them: "You feel sad right now because you want to stay up later." "You feel angry because she took your favorite spoon." "You're worried that Gramma won't be able to come to the zoo." Don't fix the situation for them; simply state the situation and the normal emotional response to help them make the connection between what's happening and the emotion that helps them deal with what's happening. Note that these statements don't try to control the child's emotions or shame them for having them; they're matter-of-fact statements about why the emotions are there.

As children develop more vocabulary, it helps to give them a sense of self-determination over their emotions; at a certain point, you should stop naming their emotions for them and instead ask them about which emotions they're feeling. (It's okay to give them hints: "Are you feeling happy? Sad? Crabby? Afraid?") It also helps to ask them why they feel specific emotions, so they can connect the emotions with the help and support the emotions are bringing to the situation.

You can also help children develop their emotional vocabulary by teaching them many words for each emotion at every level of intensity (see the Emotional Vocabulary Lists in chapter 2 or find a free downloadable version online at karlamclaren.com/wp-content/uploads/2016/05/Emotional-Vocabulary-List-Color.pdf).

For instance, with anxiety, you can help children feel and identify anxiety levels from soft and quiet to big and powerful with the words *fidgety, uneasy, worried, nervous, anxious,* and *overwhelmed.* There are, of course, many other words for anxiety, but these are ones that children may understand.

Researcher Lisa Feldman Barrett and her colleagues found that simply having a larger and more precise emotional vocabulary helps people develop better emotional regulation all by itself.[1] A large and healthy vocabulary is vital to emotional health, so make a habit of developing your own large emotional vocabulary and sharing it with children.

The following excerpt is from the children's book I'm working on now, *Emotions! The Smart Kid's Field Guide to the Wonderful World of Feelings*. I use the word *worry* instead of *anxiety* because it's a more accessible word for small children.

Worry helps you figure out how to plan for the future. What do you need to do to get ready? What needs to happen first, second, and third?

Worry also warns you when you're putting off an important job. It's time to get to work!

How can you help your worry?

First, breathe! Worry has a lot of energy, and sometimes, it can feel like too much energy!

Take a slow breath in through your nose, counting 1, 2, 3, 4.

Then breathe out slowly through your mouth, counting 1, 2, 3, 4, 5, 6.

Your breathing will help you calm down so that you can focus yourself. When you can focus, talk to someone about your worries, and ask them to help you write down what you need to do. Worry is trying to help you.

Worry brings you the energy you need to plan ahead and do your best. Worry helps you figure out all of the possible problems so that you'll be ready for anything.

Worry brings you the energy you need to pay attention, plan for the future, and get your work done. Breathe in and out slowly, make a plan, and help your worry help you get ready!

PLAYING WITH YOUR WORRY

You can play pretend games with your worry and learn how to plan ahead and get lots of things done on time:

1. Pretend that you have to clean your room if you want to go camping this weekend, but you keep putting it off and off and off. Ask your worry to help you get moving!

2. Imagine that you have a test at school, a baseball game, and a birthday party happening tomorrow, and you don't feel ready at all. What do you feel? What help do you need? Who could help you plan?

3. Pretend that you have to do a ridiculously hard job, like building a working bicycle out of marshmallows. Where do you start? Who could help you?

When you can help your worry, it will help you plan ahead, work smart, and be ready for what's coming next. Thank you, worry!

Notes

INTRODUCING MY FRIEND ANXIETY

1. This expanded definition references the root of our English word *empathy*, which formally entered our language in 1908 as a translation of the German word *Einfühlung*. *Einfühlung* means "in-feeling" or "feeling into" and was used by members of the German aesthetic movement of the late nineteenth century as a way to explore the expression of emotion into artworks by the artist and the reception of emotion from the artwork by the viewer, listener, or reader. *Einfühlung* is not limited to human relationships, and neither is its namesake, *empathy*. See my book *The Art of Empathy* (Boulder, CO: Sounds True, 2013) for a further discussion of *Einfühlung*.

CHAPTER 1: EMBRACING THE FORESIGHT AND
FOCUS OF ANXIETY

1. The fighting, fleeing, and freezing responses in panic are not the only ones. Many observers have noted that there is also a *flooding* response, where a person is overwhelmed by intense emotions, and a *fawning* or *friending* response, where an endangered person learns to either appease or befriend an abuser as a way to survive. There are other panic responses listed in various emotion theories, but these five are the ones most people focus on. No matter how many panic responses there turn out to be, however, it's important to know that all of them are genius-level responses that may ensure survival in the face of threats and traumas.

2. HelpGuide (helpguide.org) is an essential site created by the late sociologist and psychologist Jeanne Segal, PhD, and her husband, Robert Segal, after they lost their daughter Morgan Leslie Segal to suicide. The Segals felt that if Morgan had been able to access clear information about her symptoms and options, she might have survived. This site has become my go-to destination for well-written, well-researched, and calming information about mental health conditions and social and emotional health.

3. You can listen to the archived interview with Dr. Lamia on the *Forum* web page "Emotional Kids" (kqed.org/forum/201012071000 /emotional-kids).

4. I wrote about my better understanding of anxiety in my 2013 book, *The Art of Empathy*, and I welcomed anxiety into the group of seventeen emotions (it was sixteen before I added anxiety) that I feature in my Dynamic Emotional Integration® process (DEI for short). Dr. Lamia went on to write a book about anxiety and emotions in 2017: *What Motivates Getting Things Done: Procrastination, Emotions, and Success* (Rowman & Littlefield), and it's a wonderful support for everyone, but especially for the deadline-focused procrastinators who are almost always shamed about their (excellent and useful) motivational style. If you want to learn more about your own motivational style and how to work with it, it's a very helpful book.

5. Task-focused people may not be able to relax or stop working because there are always more tasks to do. Dr. Lamia also notes that in their rush to complete things far ahead of deadlines, task-focused people can create finished jobs that aren't very carefully done — though they will at least be complete. Deadline-focused people, on the other hand, tend to enjoy their free time because they tend not to experience the constant, unending call to finish everything that task-focused people do.

6. In psychology, psychiatry, and neurology, *valencing* is a simplistic separation of emotions into two categories: *positive* (pleasant, pro-social) and *negative* (unpleasant, antisocial). Negatively valenced emotions are generally the uncomfortable or unwanted ones, and positively valenced emotions are generally the comfortable and valued ones. When people valence emotions negatively (or positively), I always wonder: "Negative for what? Positive for whom?" In most cases,

negative emotions are the ones that shake up the status quo, while positive emotions tend to support it. Valencing is also connected to social control, such that the people who feel the positive emotions are often heard while the people who feel the negative ones are often silenced or shunned (unless the person expressing negative emotions has power; in many cases, powerful people don't face the same emotional consequences that the rest of us do).

7. Lisa Feldman Barrett and her colleagues have found that increasing your emotional "granularity," or the range of your emotional vocabulary, can increase your emotional regulation skills all by itself. Identifying your emotions with granularity can help you calm and soothe yourself so that your body knows that you're feeling anxiety, for instance, and that your increased activation does not mean that you're in danger. See T. B. Kashdan, L. Feldman Barrett, and P. E. McKnight, "Unpacking Emotion Differentiation: Transforming Unpleasant Experience by Perceiving Distinctions in Negativity," *Current Directions in Psychological Science* 24, no. 1 (2015): 10–16. Also see L. Feldman Barrett, *How Emotions Are Made: The Secret Life of the Brain* (Boston: Houghton Mifflin Harcourt, 2017).

8. Anxiety and panic attacks can be mistaken for heart attacks, but in women, anxiety symptoms may be signs of an actual heart attack! Canadian heart-attack survivor and author Carolyn Thomas created the excellent Heart Sisters website, which offers a list of women's heart attack symptoms in the article "Am I Having a Heart Attack?" (myheartsisters. org/about-women-and-heart-disease/heart-attack-sign). For instance, in some older women, heart attacks may not involve any chest pain at all. Carolyn Thomas also writes about a study that found that women under age fifty-five were often sent home from the emergency room with an anxiety diagnosis when they were actually having a heart attack. See her article "When Your Doctor Mislabels You as an 'Anxious Female'" (myheartsisters.org/2012/06/04/anxious-female).

CHAPTER 2: MEETING YOUR FOUR EMOTION FAMILIES

1. For a deeper dive into the emotions, my book *The Language of Emotions: What Your Feelings Are Trying to Tell You* (Boulder, CO: Sounds True, 2010) will give you a fuller picture. For a quicker overview,

The Dynamic Emotional Integration® Workbook (Windsor, CA: Laughing Tree, 2018) is a hands-on workbook. There are also many online courses devoted to the emotions at my learning site, Empathy Academy (empathyacademy.org), where you can learn about emotions and empathy in a welcoming community.

2. Shadow work is a self-awareness and integration practice first developed by Carl Jung. Shadow work helps people address their hatred intentionally so that they can detoxify and integrate hated behaviors into their whole selves. Shadow work is also helpful for infatuation or idolization, which, like hatred, are dehumanizing. See "Recommended Resources" at the end of this book for suggested books on the shadow.

3. Suicide lifeline in the **United States**: Call the National Suicide Prevention Lifeline at 1-800-273-8255 or visit their website at suicidepreventionlifeline.org.

   Canada: See a listing of support centers at the Canadian Association for Suicide Prevention website at suicideprevention.ca/survivor -support-centres.

   Internationally: See the International Association for Suicide Prevention website for a list of crisis centers worldwide at iasp.info /index.php.

4. See note 3 above.

5. The hypothesis that sleep prunes intense emotions from memories is under investigation, but the research is not following people over time or focusing on naturalistic emotional memories. For the original hypothesis, see M. P. Walker and E. van der Helm, "Overnight Therapy? The Role of Sleep in Emotional Brain Processing," *Psychological Bulletin* 135, no. 5 (2009): 731–748, doi:10.1037/a0016570.

CHAPTER 3: MINDFULNESS PRACTICES FOR NURTURING YOUR EMOTIONAL GENIUS

1. I developed these practices over four decades, and I continue to modify and simplify them as I go. The first five practices are from my book *The Language of Emotions: What Your Feelings Are Trying to Tell You* (Boulder, CO: Sounds True, 2010), and I added the Resourcing practice in *The Art of Empathy: A Complete Guide to Life's Most*

Essential Skill (Boulder, CO: Sounds True, 2013). The shortened and simplified versions of the practices in this book are excerpted from *The Dynamic Emotional Integration® Workbook* (Windsor, CA: Laughing Tree, 2018).

2. As a personal note, I developed these practices when I was a deeply dissociated and emotionally volatile young person running on the fumes of childhood trauma and major depression. I developed these skills to address the severe destabilization I experienced in the hope that I could rebuild my life from scratch. It worked, but I won't lie to you: some of these skills were *hard* at first. Now, they're second nature, and I don't even have to think about them. If you have any difficulties, I empathize. I also know after teaching these practices for over three decades that healing and reintegration are not just possible, but likely.

3. This sense of personal space is an aspect of your physical awareness, your balance, and your capacity for coordinated movement in three-dimensional space. It's called your *proprioceptive* awareness, and your brain and your nervous system map it in every moment so that you'll know where you are and what kind of movement is physically possible and safe for you. A wonderful book on your proprioceptive system is Sandra and Matthew Blakeslee's *The Body Has a Mind of Its Own* (New York: Random House, 2008).

4. Research on positive affirmations, positive relationship behaviors, and positivity in general is not positive. See J. K. McNulty, "When Positive Processes Hurt Relationships," *Current Directions in Psychological Science* 19, no. 3 (2010): 167–171; J. V. Wood, W. Q. E. Perunovic, and J. W. Lee, "Positive Self-Statements: Power for Some, Peril for Others," *Psychological Science* 20, no. 7 (2009): 860–866; and M. Szalavitz, "Why Swearing Sparingly Can Help Kill Pain," *Time Magazine*, November 23, 2011, healthland.time.com/2011/11/23/why-swearing-sparingly-can-help-kill-pain.

5. There is also a Conscious Complaining with a Partner practice that's a wonderful thing to teach your friends and family. See my book *The Art of Empathy* (Boulder, CO: Sounds True, 2013). These practices are based on the skills Hard Times and the Private Gripe in the book *Wishcraft* by the marvelous Barbara Sher (New York: Ballantine Books, 1979).

6. You can learn more about Dr. Peter Levine's trauma-healing work and his many books and audio learning programs at his website trauma-healing.org.

7. A wonderful sleep book to read, especially if your anxiety gets involved with your sleep issues, is W. Chris Winter's *The Sleep Solution: Why Your Sleep Is Broken and How to Fix It* (New York: Penguin/Random House, 2017). Dr. Winter is a funny and calming sleep doctor who helps you understand what sleep is and how to support it, and he doesn't scare the life out of you about the downsides to sleeplessness. My insomnia-based anxiety (*anxomnia?*) appreciates Dr. Winter.

CHAPTER 5: THE DIFFERENCE BETWEEN FEAR, CONFUSION, PANIC, AND ANXIETY

1. See the classic book that introduced the topic of emotional labor, *The Managed Heart: Commercialization of Human Feeling* by Dr. Arlie Russell Hochschild (Berkeley: University of California Press, 1983).

2. See E. J. Masicampo and R. F. Baumeister, "Consider It Done! Plan Making Can Eliminate the Cognitive Effects of Unfulfilled Goals," *Journal of Personality and Social Psychology* 101, no. 4 (2011): 667.

3. See G. A. Radvansky, S. A. Krawietz, and A. K. Tamplin, "Walking Through Doorways Causes Forgetting: Further Explorations." *The Quarterly Journal of Experimental Psychology* 64, no. 8 (2011): 1632–1645; and G. A. Radvansky and J. M. Zacks, "Event Boundaries in Memory and Cognition," *Current Opinion in Behavioral Sciences* 17 (2017): 133–140.

4. I was diagnosed with ADHD when I was a child (it was called hyperactivity then). Ritalin was suggested, but it was being given in very large doses then, which had a sedating effect. My mother was not having any of that, so she helped me learn to work with all of the energy I had. I was fortunate to grow up in a family of brilliantly atypical people who created an environment where our differences were welcome. I still have the same amount of energy and wide, bouncing focus today as I did when I was a child, but I've learned to work with and solve for my divergence from the norm. I also created the Empathic Mindfulness practices specifically to help me work with the energy I have and the neurology I inherited. Attention-focusing medications can be

supportive (now that they're being given in more careful dosages) and so can learning to curate your unique neurology so that you can explore and develop your wide-angle focus. *Note*: My colleague Nick Walker has coined a new term for ADD and ADHD: *kinetic learning style* (or *kinetic cognitive style*). This is a truer and more functional title and a more effective and empathic way to approach this condition; if you've got it, welcome to the kinetic community!

5. There are other panic responses besides the big three (see note 1 for chapter 1), but I'm focusing on the big three in this chapter to make things simpler.

6. Anxioneer Jeanette Brynn is a DEI trainer and consultant from Washington State who created the mixed-emotion word *fleezing*, which is a fleeing and freezing response. When you *fleeze*, you stay perfectly still while your awareness hightails it outta there! You may have experienced this when you're asked a question in a high-stakes situation, and though you're still physically present, your mind and your ability to form words completely abandon ship. I also experienced my dissociative responses to childhood trauma as *fleezing* responses; I was still present in the room, and very still, but my awareness flew away to safety.

CHAPTER 6: ATTENDING TO PANIC AND ANXIETY

1. Somatic therapies can be supportive, and I used Peter Levine's Somatic Experiencing® process (along with my own Empathic Mindfulness practices) to address my own dissociative tendencies. However, the field is holding on to outdated or disconfirmed ideas such as the triune brain theory or the polyvagal hypothesis, so I want you to know that there is a lack of research to support this field. Also, while many people swear by somatic approaches, they don't help everyone. Cognitive therapies such as cognitive behavioral therapy have better research support for certain conditions (though there's a great deal of conflict about what this research support actually means), but they also don't help everyone. The best outcomes, regardless of modality, tend to occur when the therapist is empathic and engaged, and when the client is comfortable and dedicated to the process. For responsible and updated information about your therapeutic options, see the HelpGuide website (helpguide.org).

CHAPTER 8: DOING YOUR BEST WORK WITH SHAME AND ANXIETY

1. In DEI, we see abusive shaming messages as contracts, certainly, but we also see them as aspects of your unique heroic journey. I have seen over the decades that each of us picks up specific aspects of abusive messages as a survival tactic. It is often smarter to agree to some abusive messages than it is to fight all of them and endanger yourself. Part of the process of releasing these painful messages is to recognize and honor the survival skills of the person you were when you agreed to them. There is a DEI practice called the Shame Shrine that can help when your shame is acting in service to abusive messages. You can find licensed DEI consultants who know how to work with shame shrines at the Emotion Dynamics site (emotiondynamics.org/all-dei-consultants).

2. Shame and guilt are classified as *self-conscious* emotions that have an important role in social awareness, behavioral self-management, and the development of empathy. Though shame is often demonized, notice that diagnoses that involve a lack of empathy also involve a lack of shame. Shamelessness is not a valuable condition! See J. Decety, "The Neurodevelopment of Empathy in Humans," *Developmental Neuroscience* 32, no. 4 (2010): 257–267; and P. Muris et al., "Lack of Guilt, Guilt, and Shame: A Multi-informant Study on the Relations Between Self-Conscious Emotions and Psychopathology in Clinically Referred Children and Adolescents," *European Child & Adolescent Psychiatry* 25, no. 4 (2016): 383–396.

3. I realize that *shanxiety* is a more valid way of combining these two words, but *shmanxiety* makes me laugh. It feels like something a Borscht Belt comedian would say, and when your shame is active, it's good to keep your sense of humor about you!

CHAPTER 10: BALANCING THE HAPPINESS FAMILY AND ANXIETY

1. See the book I coauthored with cult expert (and fellow cult survivor) Dr. Janja Lalich: *Escaping Utopia: Growing Up in a Cult, Getting Out, and Starting Over* (New York: Routledge, 2017).

2. Jack Kornfield, *After the Ecstasy, the Laundry: How the Heart Grows Wise on the Spiritual Path* (New York: Bantam, 2000).

CHAPTER 11: WHEN ANXIETY IS A VITAL TOOL IN YOUR CAREER (AND YOUR LIFE)

1. See W. Chris Winter's book *The Sleep Solution: Why Your Sleep Is Broken and How to Fix It* (New York: Berkley, 2017). Dr. Winter is a down-to-earth and nonalarmist sleep doctor who can help you understand your sleep and reduce some of your anxiety about it. I read his book when I was having a bout of insomnia, and while other sleep books filled me with dread about my sleeplessness (plus visions of impending diseases, *thanks*), Dr. Winter helped me relax and get my sleep back in order.

APPENDIX: HELPING CHILDREN EMBRACE THEIR ANXIETY

1. See note 7 for chapter 1.

Recommended Resources

Emotional Support and Awareness

The Art of Empathy: A Complete Guide to Life's Most Essential Skill by Karla McLaren (Boulder, CO: Sounds True, 2013).

The Body Has a Mind of Its Own by Sandra Blakeslee and Matthew Blakeslee (New York: Random House, 2007).

The Dynamic Emotional Integration® Workbook by Karla McLaren (Windsor, CA: Laughing Tree Press, 2018).

Emotion: The Science of Sentiment by Dylan Evans (New York: Oxford University Press, 2002).

Emotional Flow Online Course (2012). Karla McLaren. Boulder CO: Sounds True. This course is offered twice per year at Empathy Academy's online learning site (empathyacademy.org).

Empathy Academy's online learning site offers courses on emotions, empathy, and self-care and a licensing program for people who wish to become Dynamic Emotional Integration® professionals. See empathyacademy.org.

Happiness: The Science Behind Your Smile by Daniel Nettle (New York: Oxford University Press, 2006).

The Happiness Myth: The Historical Antidote to What Isn't Working Today by Jennifer Michael Hecht (New York: HarperOne, 2007).

HelpGuide is a website that contains valuable and accessible information about mental and emotional health, plus comprehensive suggestions to help you find support. See helpguide.org.

How Emotions Are Made: The Secret Life of the Brain by Lisa Feldman Barrett (New York: Houghton Mifflin Harcourt, 2017).

The Language of Emotions: What Your Feelings Are Trying to Tell You by Karla McLaren (Boulder, CO: Sounds True, 2010).

The Managed Heart: Commercialization of Human Feeling by Arlie Russell Hochschild (Berkeley: University of California Press, 1983).

Understanding Myself: A Kid's Guide to Intense Emotions and Strong Feelings by Mary Lamia (Washington, DC: Magination Press, 2010).

What Motivates Getting Things Done: Procrastination, Emotions, and Success by Mary Lamia (Lanham, MD: Rowman & Littlefield, 2017).

"Your Emotional Vocabulary List" is a free pdf on the author's website that contains the entire alphabetized list of emotional vocabulary words organized by emotion and intensity. You can download the list at karlamclaren.com/wp-content/uploads/2016/05/Emotional-Vocabulary-List-Color.pdf.

Shadow Work (for Addressing Hatred and Idolization)

The Essential Jung edited by Anthony Storr (New York: MJ Books, 1983).

The Essential Rumi translated by Coleman Barks (San Francisco: HarperSanFrancisco, 1995).

A Little Book on the Human Shadow by Robert Bly (San Francisco: HarperSanFrancisco, 1988).

Meeting the Shadow: The Hidden Power of the Dark Side of Human Nature edited by Connie Zweig and Jeremiah Abrams (New York: Tarcher Putnam, 1991).

Owning Your Own Shadow by Robert Johnson (San Francisco: HarperSanFrancisco, 1993).

The Rag and Bone Shop of the Heart: A Poetry Anthology edited by Robert Bly, James Hillman, and Michael Meade (New York: Harper Perennial, 1992).

The Scapegoat Complex: Toward a Mythology of Shadow and Guilt by Sylvia Brinton Perera (Toronto: Inner City Books, 1983).

Sleep Support

The Promise of Sleep: A Pioneer in Sleep Medicine Explores the Vital Connection Between Health, Happiness, and a Good Night's Sleep by William Dement (New York: Dell, 1999).

The Sleep Solution: Why Your Sleep Is Broken and How to Fix It by W. Chris Winter (New York: New American Library, 2017).

Trauma Healing

The Boy Who Was Raised as a Dog and Other Stories from a Child Psychiatrist's Notebook: What Traumatized Children Can Teach Us About Loss, Love, and Healing by Bruce D. Perry and Maia Szalavitz (New York: Basic Books, 2017).

Escaping Utopia: Growing Up in a Cult, Getting Out, and Starting Over by Janja Lalich and Karla McLaren (New York: Routledge, 2017).

The Gift of Fear: Survival Signals That Protect Us from Violence by Gavin de Becker (Boston: Little, Brown & Company, 1997).

Healing Trauma: A Step-by-Step Program for Restoring the Wisdom of the Body (online course) by Peter Levine (Boulder, CO: Sounds True, 2011).

It Won't Hurt Forever: Guiding Your Child Through Trauma (audio program) by Peter Levine (Boulder, CO: Sounds True, 2001).

Take Back Your Life: Recovering from Cults and Abusive Relationships by Janja Lalich and Madeleine Tobias (Berkeley, CA: Bay Tree Publishing, 2006).

Index

anxiety *(continued)*
  expression and, 29–32, 83–84,
    135, 158, 162
  fear and, 7, 20–21, 26, 28,
    95–103. *See also* fearxiety.
  in fearxiety, 95–103
  future focus, 6–7, 15–17, 20,
    79, 97–102. *See also* anxiety
    professionals.
  grief, supported by, 19
  Grounding and Focusing for,
    57–60, 76, 99, 110
  guilt and, 18, 66. *See also* shame.
  Hands-On Grounding for, 85,
    113, 150
  happiness and, 8, 165–175.
    See also anxappiness.
  health and, 50
  heart attacks and, 26, 215n8
  HelpGuide.org website and, 110
  interior focus, 16, 19–21, 87,
    120–121, 150–151
  journal, 7, 47–49, 57, 76–77
  joy and, 8, 89, 165–171, 178–182.
    See also joyxiety.
  in joyxiety, 178–182
  joyxiety, balancing, 179
  Lamia, Mary, 13–15, 207,
    214n4. *See also* Lamia, Mary.
  list-making, 16–17, 80–82, 103.
    See also list-making.
  loss in manipulated joy, 170–171
  love letter to, 1–8, 208
  masked by confusion, 97, 106
  motivation and, 13–14, 16. *See
    also* motivation.
  motivational style and, 13–14,
    214nn4–5. *See also* Lamia,
    Mary.
  motto for, 86, 134, 205

anxiety *(continued)*
  nervousness and, 21
  in panfusiety, 120
  panic and, 7, 11–12, 55,
    110–113, 115–130, 173.
    See also panxiety.
  in panxiety, 28, 110–113,
    115–130, 198–206
  past focus, 16, 19–20, 120–121,
    150–151
  procrastination and,
    13–15, 214n4. *See also*
    procrastination.
  professionals. *See* anxiety
    professionals.
  questions for, 40
  response to discrimination and
    exclusion, 21–22, 124–125,
    197–206
  response to inequality and
    injustice, 21–22, 52,
    124–125, 197–206
  Rejuvenation for, 69–71, 76, 150
  repression and, 29–32, 83–84,
    135, 162, 189
  Resourcing for, 71–76, 107, 150
  Resourcing with Anxiety, 73–75
  sadness and, 19
  safe spaces and, 204
  self-care. *See* self-care.
  separation, 116
  shame and, 7, 18, 55, 66,
    141–151. *See also* shmanxiety.
  in shmanxiety, 141–151, 220n3
  shrines, 4, 207
  shyness and, 21
  situational, 80, 86, 115
  sleep and, 49, 216n5, 221n1
    (chap. 11). *See also* sleep.
  social insight and, 20–22

About the Author

Karla McLaren, M.Ed., is an award-winning author, social science researcher, and empathy pioneer. Her lifelong work focuses on her grand unified theory of emotions, which revalues even the most "negative" emotions and opens startling new pathways into self-awareness, effective communication, and healthy empathy. She is the founder and CEO of Emotion Dynamics LLC and the developer of the Empathy Academy online learning site.

Her applied work, Dynamic Emotional Integration (also known as DEI) is a groundbreaking approach to emotions and empathy that reveals the genius and healing power within the emotional realm. She has taught and licensed DEI trainers and consultants worldwide.

Karla is the author of *The Dynamic Emotional Integration*® *Workbook*; *The Art of Empathy: A Complete Guide to Life's Most Essential Skill*; *The Language of Emotions. What Your Feelings Are Trying to Tell You*; and the multimedia online course *Emotional Flow: Becoming Fluent in the Language of Emotions*.

She has also written a workbook for teens with Amanda Ball, MS, *Emotional Genius for Teens: Discovering the Brilliance Inside Your Feelings*, and is developing an illustrated children's book: *Emotions! The Smart Kid's Field Guide to the Wonderful World of*

Feelings. As a social science researcher, Karla has written and edited books and studies on autism, stigma, criminology, religious communities, cults, and cult survivors.

Karla lives in Northern California with her husband, Tino Plank, RN, a nurse educator working in hospice and end-of-life care.

About Sounds True

Sounds True is a multimedia publisher whose mission is to inspire and support personal transformation and spiritual awakening. Founded in 1985 and located in Boulder, Colorado, we work with many of the leading spiritual teachers, thinkers, healers, and visionary artists of our time. We strive with every title to preserve the essential "living wisdom" of the author or artist. It is our goal to create products that not only provide information to a reader or listener but also embody the quality of a wisdom transmission.

For those seeking genuine transformation, Sounds True is your trusted partner. At SoundsTrue.com you will find a wealth of free resources to support your journey, including exclusive weekly audio interviews, free downloads, interactive learning tools, and other special savings on all our titles.

To learn more, please visit SoundsTrue.com/freegifts or call us toll-free at 800.333.9185.